Beautiful

"CREATING BEAUTY FROM THE ORDINARY"

Heidi Matson & Ann Traffie

WWW.FROMTHEHEARTMARKET.ETSY.COM
@foodfromtheheartcookbook

Credits

FOOD FROM THE HEART II – BEAUTIFUL
Copyright © 2024
by Heidi Matson and Ann Traffie
All rights reserved. No part of this book may be used or reproduced in any manner without written permission.

CREDITS:
Authors: Heidi Matson and Ann Traffie
Photographers:
Food Photography: Heidi Matson
Group Photos: Martha Harris, Pages: 2, 4, 5, 52, 60, 74.
Artwork:
www.instagram.com/abide_creative_ Anika Traffie, Pages: 8, 58, 92, 102, 105, 168
Inserts: Ann Traffie, Pages 59, 93, 103, 169.
Editor: Linda Kaiser
Designer: Heidi Matson/Ann Traffie
Proofreading: Linda Kaiser, Naomi Kaiser
Staging: Brandon Matson
Recipe Testing: My lovely daughters and our wonderful sister-in-laws.
We couldn't have finished this without these extraordinary helpers: Brandon Matson, Todd Matson, Linnea Traffie, Naomi Kaiser, Linda Kaiser, and Martha Harris.

Printed By:
FRIESENS CORPORATION
BOOKS.FRIESENS.COM
One Printers Way, Altona, Manitoba R0G 0B0
T. 866-324-6401

ISBN # 979-8-218-50941-5
Printed in CANADA
First Printing 2024

A word from the *Authors*

This book is written to our daughters, our family, and our 'cookbook' family. Our 'cookbook' family is all of you that have asked for another book from *Food From the Heart*. Our heart is that you will find inspiration and encouragement to celebrate the life God has given you, whatever it looks like; "To find beauty in the ordinary". We talk and dream about encouraging people to find their identity in Christ. Drink deep of the wells of thankfulness and forgiveness. Peace is a beauty that can't be hidden.

From our heart to yours,

Ann and Heidi

Our Mission for Book II:

- The true meaning of "Beautiful".
- Restore the art of finding "Beauty".
- Inspire "Beauty" in your heart.
- Create "Beauty" in your home.
- Share "Beauty" with others.

"…God gave beauty freely to all humanity.

He doesn't reserve a sunset for the sinless.

In fact, He calls to His lost children through

brilliant light and high mountain peaks.

He whispers to the downcast through

gently falling snow."

_ Justina Stevens - Cageless Birds - Cultivate I, Pg. 42

CONTENTS

Chapters

COOKING WITH CONFIDENCE	9
BREAKFAST/BRUNCH	23
VEGETABLES/SIDES	61
SAUCES, RUBS & MARINADES	95
FIESTA CON AMIGOS	105
CASUALLY CREATED DINNERS	127
SOMETHING SWEET	171

Inserts

BEAUTY	59
CULTIVATE YOUR HOME	93
MOTHERHOOD	103
RECIPE FOR "GRANDMA-HOOD"	169
AUTHOR'S NOTES	206

Chapter No. 1

Cooking with CONFIDENCE

The following six delicious menus are tried and true.

They are to help you cook with confidence and enjoyment!

This little guide will help you learn to prepare food in advance, pair sides with the main dish, and bring beauty to your table.

MEAL #1	HAVE A BRUNCH
MEAL #2	BRING A NEW BABY MEAL
MEAL #3	BRING A COMFORT MEAL
MEAL #4	DINNER GUESTS AFTER CHURCH
MEAL #5	TAKE IT ON A PICNIC
MEAL #6	COME FOR DINNER - FANCY

"When virtue and modesty enlighten her charms, the luster of a beautiful woman is brighter than the stars of Heaven." _Akhenaton

Have a Brunch

If you want to make someone feel special – serve them brunch. Brunches also make special occasions very personal. It takes up most of the day and it portrays an invitation to linger. I love the quote, "Brunch: a time to nourish both body and soul".

MENU

BASIL TOMATO QUICHE	53
PECAN ROLLS	37
FLUFFY FRUIT DIP	45
MINI PANCAKES	41

THE DAY BEFORE:

1) Prepare quiche, bake, cool, wrap in plastic, and refrigerate.
2) Prepare Pecan Rolls, do NOT bake, wrap in plastic, refrigerate.
3) Prepare fruit dip, cover/refrigerate.
4) Prepare pancake dough, cook 3" size pancakes, cool on rack, bag and refrigerate.

THE MORNING OF:

1) Set table, cut flowers, put on apron, light candles.
2) Bake Pecan Rolls 1 hour before event.
3) Cut fruit and arrange with dip.
4) Reheat quiche (covered) for 30 minutes on 350°, 30 minutes before event.
5) Arrange pancakes on large cookie sheet single layer. Cover with damp paper towel. Place in oven 350°, 10-15 minutes before event.

"Brunch: practicing the art of living intentionally." —AAT

Bring a NEW BABY MEAL

Thoughtful meals for new mothers should not be too spicy, or food that could cause their babies to be fussy. It's nice if it's easy to reheat. Always bring in disposable serving dishes and provide disposable plates & utensils.

MENU

Sausage Tortellini Bake	146
Fresh Bread	84
Caesar Salad	70
Raspberry Crumble Bars	186

THE DAY BEFORE:

1.) Take out sausage to thaw in refrigerator.
2.) Bake bread (optional).
3.) Make Raspberry Crumble Bars; they are better after being refrigerated overnight.
4.) Put gift together.

THE AFTERNOON OF:

1.) Make bread.
2.) Make Sausage Tortellini Bake.
3.) Make Caesar dressing.
4.) Prepare lettuce.
5.) Deliver meal.

It's totally possible to do it all in one day. The reason I break it down is; if you don't have to rush, you can still find joy in doing it. And it's not that hard to make a pan of bars after supper and put some sausage in the fridge.

"In the garden of humanity, every baby is a fresh new flower." —Debasish Mridha

 BRING A COMFORT MEAL

If someone is going through a hard time, they most likely aren't taking care of themselves, so I like to bring a good protein and at least one healthy side. It's also fun to bring an inspirational dessert. It's a good reminder that life will be sweet again. If someone has gone through a long illness – trust me on this – they need all the "beautiful" you can get in this!!

MENU

CHICKEN PIE	154
SPECIAL KALE SALAD	66
FRESH BREAD	84
CHOCOLATE CHEESECAKE BARS	195

THE DAY BEFORE:

1.) Take chicken out of freezer to thaw.
2.) Make bread (optional).
3.) Make Chocolate Cheesecake Bars. These are best when super cold.
4.) Write a card. Give a simple gift like a candle (optional).

THE AFTERNOON OF:

1.) Make chicken pie.
2.) While pie is baking, prepare kale salad.
3.) Gather your meal. Deliver. Offer to pray with them.

Buying some Artisan bread is always an option.
Always better to take a few shortcuts than miss out on blessing someone.

"Many people will walk in and out of your life, but only true friends will leave footprints on your heart." —Eleanor Roosevelt

Dinner After Church

I know I am old fashioned, but dinner after church is very important. You create a gathering place in your home where strong family bonds are formed that last a lifetime. Consider it an art, as a cook, to come home from church and pull a delicious meal out of the oven. This takes practice or good recipes. The good recipes is what I hope to give you!

MENU

LASAGNA SOUP	149
CHEESE DUNKERS	83
OLIVE GARDEN SALAD	72
CHOCOLATE CHIP COOKIE BARS	198

THE DAY BEFORE:

1.) Make soup but do not put in noodles.
2.) Make cheese blend for scooping on soup.
3.) Make salad dressing.
4.) Make Chocolate Chip Cookie Bars.
5.) Make Cheese Dunkers. Store in airtight container.

THE MORNING OF:

1.) Put soup in crockpot. Add noodles. Place on high 4 hours.
2.) Put salad ingredients together.
3.) Zap Cheese Dunkers in micro (honey butter is a must).

If you have made any of these items more than once, you will be able to make them quickly. I have made Cheese Dunkers and soup in the morning, and bars while cleaning up lunch. But remember, if you're new to this, you can enjoy each step if it's done ahead, and there might be time to feed the baby or cut fresh greenery from the yard for the table.

"In the tapestry of life, the threads of family dinners weave the tightest bonds." Unknown

Take it on a Picnic

Life is busy, we are all saying that. SO...... schedule some fun. We need friends and they need us. These sandwiches are a favorite for picnics. You can prep ahead, the guys can grill the croissants outside, its full flavor, goes with any sides, and everyone can have a good time!

MENU

BLUE RIDGE CLUB SANDWICHES	158
MOM'S JELLO	81
VEGGIE TRAY	77
CHOCOLATE PICNIC COOKIES	181

THE DAY BEFORE:

1.) Make Mom's Jello.
2.) Make Picnic Cookies.
3.) Make Basil Aioli for sandwiches.
4.) Pack up picnic basket.
5.) Make veggie dip

THE AFTERNOON OF:

1.) Cut croissants.
2.) Cut up veggies.
3.) Mix fruit into Jello.

You can easily do all of this in one afternoon. Give yourself about 2 hours. If you don't have time for the Jello to cool, you could make the Cappuccino Fluff. We love to pack the Jet boil and make fresh coffee wherever we go.

"Some old-fashioned things like fresh air and sunshine are hard to beat. In our mad rush for progress and modern improvements, let's be sure we take along with us all the old-fashioned things worthwhile."
—Laura Ingalls Wilder

COME FOR DINNER

It's your mother-in-law's birthday, you know she will be making her own birthday dinner, so you want to invite her over. You want this to be fun, yummy, beautiful, and <u>not</u> stressful. You can do that! Go Girl! The following menu will get you to that lovely dinner!

Menu

SALISBURY STEAKS	133
PERFECT MASHED POTATOES	88
CRESCENT ROLLS	87
ROASTED CARROTS	78
CHOCOLATE SKILLET CAKE	202

THE DAY BEFORE:

1.) Make Salisbury Steaks, but <u>not</u> the gravy. Fry and refrigerate.
2.) Make mashed potatoes. Refrigerate.
3.) Make dinner rolls.
4.) Make Chocolate Skillet Cake, but not the ganache or whip cream.

THE AFTERNOON OF:

1.) Set table.
2.) Make toppings for cake, frost, and put back in refrigerator.
3.) Roast carrots. Set aside.
4.) Make gravy and pour over meat.
5.) Place meat and potatoes in the oven. 350° for 45 minutes, covered.
6.) Place carrots back in oven on bottom shelf 15 minutes before eating.
This can be all done in a day but it's a long day. I would suggest boughten rolls if you have to do it in one day.

BREAKFAST

"Acceptance of whatever this day brings, is the route to joy. I want what God wants to give me." _Elizabeth Eliot

Contents:

The Brunch Sandwich	25
Darling Dutch Babies	26
Migas Supreme (Mexican Scrambled Eggs)	29
Overnight French Toast	30
No-Bake Granola	33
Smoothie Bowls	34
Pecan Rolls	37
Running Balls	38
School Pancakes	41
Sweet potato Feta Bowls	42
Fluffy Fruit Dip	45
Blueberry Strata	46
Apple Pie Scones	49
Egg Bites	50
Tomato Basil Quiche	53
Pop Tarts	54
Breakfast Fusion	56

The Brunch Sandwich

Once, when I went with Dave to the World of Concrete, he Price-Lined a room, and we stayed on the 18th floor on the Cosmopolitan. In the mall on the first floor was a little French bakery that sold three different breakfast sandwiches. Everything we ate there was beautiful and delicious. This sandwich was our favorite; we have been recreating it for the last five years.

Heat Griddle	Serves 4

Ingredients:

4 large (6") croissants
8 eggs
8 slices American cheese
8 slices bacon

Butter for grilling

1.) Heat griddle.
2.) Cook bacon. Set aside.
3.) Wipe off griddle.
4.) Cut open croissants. Butter both cut sides. Toast the outside and the cut sides. Place on plates with cut side down.
5.) Fry eggs. For easier eating, I pop the yolks. After you flip the eggs while cooking, put one slice of cheese on each egg.
6.) Place two eggs on the bottom side of each croissant. Add three slices of bacon.
7.) Close the sandwich and cut in half. The cut side of the croissant should be on the outside.

NOTES:

- If you are transporting these sandwiches, wrap in paper towel and then parchment paper or foil. The paper towel absorbs the moisture, so they won't be soggy. (I was always looking for meal ideas to bring the guys while building our house.)
- You can use any meat you want but bacon adds nice crunchy texture.
- Costco makes the best croissants outside of a good bakery.
- Regular grocery store croissants may only be big enough for one egg.
- Croissants freeze perfectly, thaw at room temperature.

"Great minds talk about ideas; average minds talk about events; small minds talk about people." _Eleanor Roosevelt

DARLING DUTCH BABIES

Friday is Payday! Well, even if it's not, there is something great about Fridays! We homeschool, and by Friday I'm about ready to put math and spelling aside and have an art class, or cooking class, or do a fun project. The Darling Dutch Babies are a great way to start one of these Fridays. Little efforts are never wasted. When I listen to my grownup kids talk, it renews my energy to know that they remember so many special times.

| Heat oven 425° - Bake 12-14 Minutes | Makes 12 |

Ingredients:
- ¾ cup flour
- ¾ cup whole milk
- 5 eggs
- 2 TBSP honey
- ¼ cup melted butter
- 1 tsp vanilla

- 3 TBSP butter
- Powdered sugar for dusting

Toppings:
- Syrup
- Fresh Fruit
- Whip Cream
- Drizzled Nutella and Bananas

1.) Heat oven (rack on middle shelf).
2.) In blender, put: flour, milk, eggs, honey, melted butter, and vanilla. Blend just till smooth.
3.) Divide 3 TBSP butter into 12 pieces. Place in muffin tins in hot oven. Melt butter till hot and starting to turn brown.
4.) Pour batter into hot muffin tin. Divide dough evenly.
5.) Bake till golden brown.
6.) Dust with powdered sugar.
7.) Serve immediately.

NOTES:
- It is normal for there to be a little standing butter when finished baking. It is also normal for the Dutch babies to shrink while cooling.

"Right now, you are tired. Rest assured; God is not." _@thepaigepippin

"If you love a good and delicious Mexican dish, this will be your new favorite!"

Brother Kevin – Watertown, SD

Migas Supreme
(Mexican Scrambled Eggs)

When Heidi said, "We have to have 'Migas' in our next cookbook," I was like, "What is that?" Well, now I know what it is, and it's one of my new favorites. It's just full of flavor and texture and protein. I love when either one of us makes something good, we immediately have to tell each other. Heidi started that a few years ago. She said, "When I see something pretty, I just buy two, because I know Ann needs one."

Heat 9" skillet	Serves 4-6

Ingredients:

- 2 TBSP butter
- 5 corn tortillas (cut 1" squares)

- 1 TBSP butter
- 1/3 cup green pepper finely chopped
- 1/3 cup white onion, diced

- 8 eggs
- 1/3 cup heavy cream
- ½ tsp salt
- ½ tsp pepper
- ½ tsp garlic powder

- ¾ cup Mexican shredded cheese

1.) Cut tortillas 1" squares. Melt butter in skillet and toast tortillas till crispy. Set aside.
2.) Melt butter in skillet and sauté green pepper and onion till softened. Set aside.
3.) Beat eggs with cream, salt, pepper, and garlic powder.
4.) In a large hot skillet, start scrambling eggs. When half cooked add tortillas and veggies. Finish cooking and scrambling all together. Stir in cheese.
5.) Serve with toppings of your choice. We have listed our favorites.

NOTES:

- Our favorite toppings are: Avocado chunks, Cilantro, Salsa Verde, Roma tomatoes, & Jalapeno Slices.
- Serve Immediately. Do not make ahead.

"Life doesn't have to be perfect to be beautiful!" _AT

Overnight French Toast

We often celebrate big things, but what is really special is when we celebrate little things. When we celebrate little things, we are really celebrating the person. This creates great relationships and family ties. There won't be many people in your life that serve you breakfast in bed just because it's the first Saturday you haven't worked in a month. Celebrate!

Heat oven 375° - 30 minutes - Uncovered	Makes 9x13

Ingredients:
1 large loaf French bread

12 eggs
2 cups whole milk
2 TBSP maple syrup
½ tsp salt
1 TBSP vanilla extract
½ tsp allspice

Crumble Topping:
2/3 cup butter
¾ cup flour
¾ cup almond flour
½ cup brown sugar
¼ tsp salt
1 tsp vanilla
2 tsp cinnamon

Maple Syrup

1.) Cut bread into 1" slices and then 1" cubes. Place in greased 9x13.
2.) Whisk together: eggs, milk, syrup, salt, vanilla, and allspice.
3.) Pour over bread.
4.) CRUMBLE TOPPING: butter needs to be room temperature or softened 30 seconds in micro. Mix all topping ingredients with a pastry blender or with your fingers. Sprinkle over French toast.
5.) Cover and refrigerate. Minimum of 1 hour or overnight.
6.) Bake uncovered.
7.) Dust with powdered sugar.
8.) Serve with syrup.

NOTES:
- This recipe pairs well with egg bites or quiche.
- I love to make this on Saturday night. Get up Sunday morning and put in the oven before my shower. By the time you are dressed the kitchen smells amazing.

"Happiness in letting go of what you think your life should look like and celebrate it for everything that it is." _Mandy Hale

"A fun new twist on this recipe with the crumble topping. I love the Allspice. Having breakfast ready sure helped our Sunday morning rush!"
Kaylyn Traffie – Watertown, SD

No-Bake Granola
CHOCOLATE PEANUT-BUTTER

No-bake granola is soft and chewy. It is named after the No-Bake cookie, but we do bake it. When my daughter was expecting her first baby, she called and said, "What's that one granola recipe, Mom, I am just craving it"! This can be stored in an airtight container at room temperature for two months.

Stovetop – Bake 350º 20 Minutes.	Yields appx. 7 cups

Ingredients:

½ cup butter
1 cup brown sugar
1-1/2 cups peanut butter
1 cup chocolate protein powder
1 tsp salt

5 cups oats

1.) In a large saucepan, melt butter.
2.) Stir in brown sugar till melted.
3.) Add peanut butter, protein powder, and salt. Stir till smooth.
4.) Add oats. Stir till combined.
5.) Spread on cookie sheet. Bake 20 minutes.
6.) Set aside until completely cool.
7.) Store in an air-tight container.
8.) You can store at room temperature or in refrigerator up to one month.

NOTES:

You can substitute the chocolate protein powder for 1/3 cup baking cocoa. It doesn't change the flavor much and definitely helps the budget.

You can also add coconut, slivered almonds, pumpkin seeds, or add-ins of your choice.

"Help your brain process with the unprocessed." _Unknown

Smoothie Bowls

My introduction to acai bowls was Alissa's wedding. My niece Karmyn asked if she could bring our family "wedding breakfast" on wedding day. This was more special than I can describe. "Wedding breakfast" is now a tradition, and acai bowls are a new favorite. I call them "smoothie bowls" because I don't usually use acai. It's expensive and hard to find in large quantities. This recipe increases the protein content for a hardier breakfast.

| Good blender | Serves 6 |

Ingredients:

2 bananas
2 cups frozen blueberries
2 cups frozen strawberries
½ cup vanilla protein powder
1 avocado
½ cup milk

Toppings:

Strawberries
Bananas
Blueberries
Melted peanut butter
Granola
Coconut
Slivered almonds
Whip Cream

1.) Prepare toppings first. Slice fruit, melt peanut butter, place other items in small bowls.
2.) In blender place bananas, blueberries, strawberries, protein powder, avocado, and milk. Blend till smooth.
3.) Dish out into small bowls and serve immediately.
4.) If preparing ahead of time, place in individual serving size containers. Freeze.

NOTES:

- Prepare ahead and freeze, as far in advance as necessary.
- For immediate use from the freezer, microwave 30 seconds.
- Yogurt is a great way to add protein, but do not add yogurt if refreezing, the texture is bad.
- In the picture we did Honey Dew balls.

"The best thing to hold onto in life, is each other." _Audrey Hepburn

READERS CHOICE:
"Pecan rolls are just what I need to welcome my family in from morning chores on the farm; to the taste and smell of home, I hope they will always remember." Sonya Keranen – Wolf Lake, Minnesota

Pecan Rolls

There is this vivid memory from our childhood, it goes like this: Saturday morning, Pacific Northwest drizzle, Multnomah Falls Lodge, sitting in the 'Falls Room', looking out the big windows, There was dad and mom and all us kids, Hot chocolate, Large yellow Maple leaves falling (like 8"-10" leaves), and there was PECAN ROLLS! We did this often.

Preheat oven 350º, Bake 24-25 minutes.	Yields: 15 rolls 9x13

Dough:
1 cup warm milk
½ cup butter
1/3 cup sugar
2 eggs
4 tsp instant yeast
1 tsp salt
4 cups flour

In bottom of pan:
2/3 cup brown sugar
2 TBSP honey
½ cup butter
¾ cup chopped pecans

Filling:
5 TBSP butter
¾ cup brown sugar
1-1/2 TBSP cinnamon

1.) DOUGH: in microwave safe bowl place milk, butter, and sugar. High for 2 minutes. Whisk in eggs and yeast. Let rest for 5 minutes.
2.) In standup mixer place warm wet ingredients, salt, and flour. Let knead 5 minutes.
3.) Place in 200º oven for 10 minutes. Let rise till dough is almost double. While rising-
4.) Mix all ingredients for caramel layer in a small saucepan. Almost bring to a boil. Pour in bottom of 9x13 pan. Sprinkle with pecans.
5.) Roll out dough about 12"x15"
6.) Spread filling ingredients.
7.) Roll up (should be 15" long roll)
8.) Cut in 1" circles layer in pan 3 across and 5 long.
9.) <u>LET RISE</u> 30 minutes.
10.) Bake. Let sit 5 minutes before inverting.

NOTES:
- To make in advance: Cover and refrigerate, up to one day before. When you want to bake them: let stand at room temperature 30-45 minutes before baking. Bake longer than above as dough is cold. 26-28 minutes.
- Recipe tested in a 9x13 glass pan (metal pans vary in baking time). Internal temperature of 182º-185º degrees in the middle rolls.

"Nothing can substitute spending time with your kids." _AT

Running Balls

Family staple right here. Mix and match ingredients and keep a batch on hand at all times. These are great for pre-workouts, breakfast on the go, toddler snacks, and best of all race day!! Being active is a blessing, not a punishment. It's worth the effort to have healthy snacks, cute water bottles, good running shoes, and a good exercise buddy. Right NOW, my running buddies are most often three toddlers on bikes. The conversation is not great, but they grow up quickly and I cherish the time of all these little ones around me.

Freeze	Makes 30 Pieces

Ingredients:
½ cup peanut butter
½ cup butter
2-3/4 cups oats
½ cup honey
1 cup chocolate protein powder
¼ cup chia seeds
¼ cup ground flax
1 cup Rice Krispies
½ cup chocolate chips
½ tsp sea salt

1.) Place all ingredients in mixer. Mix till combined like cookie dough.
2.) Line freezer container with wax paper. Form balls with cookie scoop. Cover and freeze.
3.) Wrap in plastic wrap or sandwich bags for run day.

NOTES:
- May use collagen instead of protein powder.
- May use coconut instead of chia and flax.
- I use Vital Proteins protein powder (goes on sale at Costco and Sam's), and it tastes good.
- You can have fun with the combinations.

"You don't stop running because you get old, you get old because you stop running!" _Christopher McDougall

"My favorite school breakfast is these pancakes and iced coffee.
I make the batter the night before, then its easy to make them in the morning."
Arianna Traffie – Age 11

School Pancakes

I read something many years ago that changed my thinking on teaching and therefore my personal eating, "It's not what you teach, but how you teach." That goes for anything in our lives. Anyway, I tend to get low blood sugar and that in turn makes me a moody teacher. I really strive for high protein breakfasts so I can stay calm throughout the day. Harsh words can so quickly damage a student's love for learning.

Heat Griddle/Frying Pan 250º	Makes (24) 5-6" pancakes

Batter:
- 8 eggs
- 2 cups cottage cheese
- 1 cup plain Greek yogurt
- ¾ cup milk
- ¼ cup honey (or sugar)
- 1 TBSP vanilla

- 2-1/2 cups whole wheat flour
- ¾ tsp salt
- 1 tsp baking powder
- 1 tsp baking soda

1.) Place all ingredients in blender.
2.) Pulse.
3.) Cook on buttered griddle.
4.) When bubbles start to form, flip and finish cooking the other side.
5.) Serve hot with butter and syrup.

NOTES:
- When freezing pancakes for make ahead breakfasts, cool completely. Layer with wax paper between. Reheat with toaster or microwave between two plates (top plate upside-down).
- Each pancake is 9-10 grams of protein per serving. Your student won't be getting sugar blues during class.

"Education is what remains after one has forgotten what one has learned in school!" _Albert Einstein

Sweet Potato Feta Bowls

Amazing, beautiful, healthy, brunches, suppers, vegetarian…..How much should we brag up this not so traditional dish? Just give it a try. To speed this up for morning, I usually use leftover sweet potatoes from supper the night before. Sweet potatoes grow in the dirt so they are full of all kinds of vitamins, antioxidants, fiber, and stuff we need. If you are not a Feta cheese lover, try plain Cotija, it's a crumbly Mexican cheese with very mild flavor.

Heat oven 425º - 35 minutes - Uncovered	Makes 6 bowls

Potatoes:
- 3 large sweet potatoes
- 2 TBSP oil
- ½ tsp salt, after roasting
- ½ tsp coarse pepper
- ½ tsp garlic powder

Bowls:
- ½ lb. ground sausage
- 1 TBSP butter
- 1/3 cup chopped green pepper
- 1/3 cup chopped onion
- 3 cups chopped kale
- 6 oz. Feta cheese
- 12 eggs scrambled
- ¾ tsp salt
- ½ tsp coarse pepper
- 2/3 cup whole milk
- 1 TBSP butter (for the pan)

1.) POTATOES: Start the potatoes first. Wash. Cut in ½" x 1" cubes (I don't peel). Place on parchment lined baking sheet. Drizzle oil over potatoes and toss with your hands to coat. Bake uncovered 35 minutes. Season potatoes after cooking to help ensure crispiness.

2.) Brown sausage. Drain. Set aside.

3.) VEGGIES: In skillet, melt butter, sauté green pepper and onions five minutes, add kale. Sauté only until kale starts to wilt.

4.) EGGS: beat 12 eggs, add salt, pepper, and milk. Whisk. Melt butter in hot skillet. Spread butter over bottom and sides of the pan. Scramble.

5.) Assemble bowls: sweet potatoes in the bottom, sausage, veggies, 2 eggs, 1 oz feta (crumbled).

NOTES:
- The Cotija (kuh-tee-huh) cheese mentioned above is found in the Hispanic cooler section. It's reasonably priced and you can put it on anything. It is like an extra, extra mild version of feta.

"Never regret a day in your life: Good days give happiness, Bad days give experience, Worst days give lessons, and Best days give memories!" _Unknown

Fluffy Fruit Dip

We were dreaming up a baby shower brunch for one of my daughters, and this grandma thinks baby girls should be celebrated with a lot of pink and lace, and light, bright, beautiful things; that also includes the food at their shower. Of course we need lots of good protein, but how about some pretty pink pop-tarts, and some fluffy pink fruit dip, and maybe some strawberry lemonade? So fun! And this recipe is so easy you will be celebrating for no reason at all.

No Heat	Serves 12

Ingredients

2 cups whipping cream
½ cup powdered sugar

2 cups vanilla Greek yogurt
3 TBSP strawberry Jello

Fruit of choice: or

Strawberries
Bananas
Apples
Pineapple
Melons

1.) Beat cream in mixing bowl.
2.) Add in powdered sugar.
3.) Add vanilla yogurt and Jello and beat till smooth.
4.) Cover and refrigerate.
5.) Cut fruit and arrange on platter.
6.) Apples and bananas can only be cut 15 min before you eat them unless you dip them in orange juice, so they don't turn brown.

NOTES:

- Dip can be made one day ahead.
- You can change the flavor and color by using different Jello.

"If you think you're too small to have an impact, try going to bed with a mosquito." _Anita Roddick

Blueberry Strata

Think of this recipe as a skill more than a recipe. It's like a formula of proportions and you put in what you have or what your family eats. Of course, I will make suggestions in the following, but really, you can do this. Read the side notes on the differences in basic egg dishes, this will help you read recipes and order in restaurants with confidence.

Bake 350° Covered 30 min + 30 min uncovered.	9x13 serves 8-12

Filling:
1 loaf of French bread (1 lb. loaf)
1-1/2 cups frozen blueberries
1-1/2 (8oz.) pkg. cream cheese

12 eggs
2 cups milk
½ tsp salt
½ cup white sugar
1 tsp cinnamon
1 TBSP vanilla

Blueberry Sauce:
1 cup sugar
3 TBSP corn starch
1 cup water
1 cup blueberries
½ tsp cinnamon
1 TBSP butter

1.) Spray 9x13 pan.
2.) Cut bread into 1" cubes.
3.) Layer half of bread in pan, sprinkle blueberries.
4.) Cut cream cheese into 1-inch cubes and place over bread.
5.) Cover with remaining bread.
6.) Whisk eggs, milk, salt, and sugar. Pour over contents of pan.
7.) Cover and let sit 1 hour or up to overnight. Bake.
8.) For sauce: In a small saucepan- whisk dry sugar and cornstarch, then whisk in cold water. Bring to a boil and add blueberries and cinnamon. Boil one minute and add butter. Stir till smooth.

NOTES:

To go savory: Omit blueberries, cream cheese, and sugar.
Add in 1-1/2 cups of vegetables and 2 cups of cooked meat.

ADVICE FROM A BLUEBERRY
"Be well-rounded, Soak up the sun, Find beauty in small things,
Live a fruitful life, It's Ok to be a little blue, Make sweet memories." _Ilan Shamir

COOK WITH CONFIDENCE:

The worst thing you can do is overbake a scone. Here is a great tip for perfect baking. Set your time a couple minutes less then recommended baking time.

Do the 'wiggle' test. Quickly reach in the oven and wiggle the top of one scone. If it wiggles- it's not done. Give it one or two more minutes. Test until firm.

Apple Pie Scones

What is there not to say about this wonderful concoction? Make ahead! Freeze! Bake! Eat! I use Granny Smith apples for a very apple taste, but any kind will work. Remember when working with biscuits or scones, never bake less than 400°; if your oven is cool, turn it up 15°. A cool oven will make them go flat. Also, remember to handle your dough as little as possible. The less the butter is handled the flakier the dough. When baking, sprinkle your parchment paper with cinnamon and sugar or sugar crystals, this is more great texture!!

Preheat oven 400°, Bake 20-22 minutes.	Serves 8

Filling:
3 small green apples
2 TBSP sugar
1 pinch of salt
1-1/2 tsp cinnamon

Dough:
2-1/2 cups flour
¼ cup sugar
2 tsp baking powder
½ tsp salt
½ cup butter
2 tsp apple cider vinegar
1 egg
½ cup whole milk
¼ cup coarse sugar

Icing:
1-1/2 cup powdered sugar
4 TBSP heavy cream
½ tsp vanilla
Pinch of salt

1.) FILLING: Peel and slice apples 1/16" slices. Mix apples with sugar, salt, and cinnamon. Microwave for 3 minutes. Set aside.
2.) DOUGH: Mix together dry ingredients. Grate cold butter into dry ingredients and toss with your fingers.
3.) Whisk together vinegar, egg, and milk. Add to dry ingredients. Stir with a big spoon until combined.
4.) Dump out dough onto wax paper, knead with your hands to form a ball. Then press out dough to form 8" x 16" rectangle.
5.) Drain apples, spread over dough. Fold dough in half.
6.) Cut in fourths, cut each fourth in half-diagonally. *See Below.*
7.) Place on parchment lined pan. Sprinkle with sugar and freeze 15 minutes. Bake. Uncovered.
8.) Let cool at least 15 minutes before icing.

WHY FREEZE???
If you want LIGHT and TENDER scones, freeze them!! This returns the butter to a solid state, so they will rise and not flatten. It also lets the gluten relax for super tenderness.
- If using milk in the icing instead of cream, use 2-3 TBSP.

Egg Bites

Egg bites are personal. I really only like them by what is inside of them. When I make them for the family, I usually make two pans and one is always plain ham and cheese. We have big opinions on what is best in them. My favorite is Canadian bacon and gruyere cheese. Please use the following as a guide, and find what your favorite is.

Heat oven 325° Bake 30 minutes	Makes 12 muffins

Ingredients:

- 12 eggs
- 1/3 cup sour cream
- 1 tsp baking powder
- ½ tsp salt
- ½ tsp pepper
- ¾ cup any vegetable *(if desired)*
- 6 slices Canadian bacon *(diced small)*
- 1-1/2 cups cheddar cheese or cheese of your choice.

1.) Heat oven. Place a large cake pan in the oven with ½" warm water.
2.) Spray muffin tin with nonstick cooking spray
3.) Divide meat into muffin tin.
4.) Sauté vegetables for 3 minutes till softened. Place on top of meat. (optional)
5.) In blender: add eggs, sour cream, salt, and pepper. Blend 30 seconds. Pour evenly into muffin tin.
6.) Sprinkle with cheese.
7.) Place muffin pan in larger pan of hot water.
8.) Bake.

NOTES:

- Store up to three days in the refrigerator. Reheat in microwave.
- If you do not want the muffins to be brown on the outside, you have to use the parchment paper, or a silicone muffin pan. If your muffin pans are not fairly new, please use parchment squares. The eggs will stick. If you make a lot of muffins order the preformed parchments on Amazon.
- Best served fresh.

"If an egg is broken by outside force, life ends. If broken by an inside force, life begins. Great things always begin inside" _Jim Kwik

Tomato Basil Quiche

I love to eat outside. I think that comes from our childhood. Dad built porches literally on all sides of the house. Two of them had eating areas. So, my favorite breakfasts are outside with the morning breeze blowing softly. That's the perfect setting. When Heidi and I were talking about what's the perfect food, we said, "Pecan rolls and tomato basil quiche". My kids added, "That kinda morning would have iced coffees." See page 57 for our favorite coffee syrup.

Heat 350° - Bake 46 minutes- Uncovered	9" Deep Pie Dish – Makes 8 Slices

CRUST:
1 cup flour
¼ tsp salt
1 stick of butter (1/2 cup)
3 TBSP ice water

VEGGIES:
1 TBSP olive oil
¼ cup diced onion
2 cloves fresh garlic
1 medium zucchini, cubed

1 ball fresh mozzarella
1 (3") tomatoes
Fresh basil (no stems)

EGGS:
6 eggs
1 cup heavy cream
½ tsp salt
¼ tsp coarse black pepper

1.) Mix flour and salt. With a cheese grater, grate butter into flour. Use your fingers to crumble grated butter and flour together.
2.) Pour in water, with your fingers, work dough into a lump. Let rest 5 minutes. While resting-
3.) Heat skillet with oil. Sauté onion two minutes. Add zucchini and garlic. Sauté another 5 minutes.
4.) With your fingertips, press crust into pan (no need to roll). Place hot veggies on crust.
5.) Whisk together eggs, cream, salt and pepper. Pour over veggies.
6.) Layer thin slices of mozzarella, ¼" slices of tomato, and arrange basil leaves in fun patterns (12 leaves).
7.) Bake, uncovered, till set, about 46 minutes.
8.) Let rest 10-15 minutes before serving.

NOTES:
- For a healthier version of quiche see page 49 of Book 1.
- To make ahead: Fully cook. Cool. Wrap in plastic. Refrigerate or freeze.
- To reheat from refrigerator: let come to room temperature, cover with foil. Bake 30 minutes on 350° or (160°).
- To reheat from freezer: Place on baking sheet. Bake frozen. Cover with foil. Bake 40-45 minutes/350°. Internal temp should be 160°.

Pop-Tarts

Pop-tarts are the best example of making something "ordinary" into "beautiful". You should have all the ingredients in your pantry. The little secret is the soft dough and adding some filling to the glaze. The filling makes the beautiful color. These will be a hit at any PTA meeting, mom's group, church pot-luck, brunch, and make them for no reason, your kids won't forget.

Heat 350° Bake 25 Minutes	Makes 2 dozen

Crust:
5-1/2 cups flour
1 tsp salt
2 cups butter
2 egg yolks
1 cup evaporated milk

Filling:
2 cups blueberries
1 cup water
¾ cup sugar
2 tsp lemon juice
5 TBSP cornstarch

Glaze:
2-1/2 cups powdered sugar
5-6 TBSP milk
2-3 TBSP blueberry filling

*1 beaten egg white (acts as a seal so the filling doesn't leak)

1.) Sift together flour and salt. Grate butter into flour and crumble together with your fingers.
2.) Beat egg yolks with evaporated milk. Pour into flour. Stir to form a soft round dough ball.
3.) Divide dough into four pieces and roll into rectangles 10"x15".
4.) Use a 4" biscuit cutter, cut 12 circles for each quarter of dough.
5.) FILLING: Put all ingredients in the blender. Blend 5 seconds. Pour in saucepan. Bring to a boil. Boil 1 minute. Cool slightly.
6.) Place 1 heaping TBSP of filling on circle. *<u>Use a pastry brush and brush ½" egg white around the edge of each circle</u>. Cover with another circle. Crimp edges with a fork. Place on baking sheet with parchment paper beneath. Bake 12 per pan. Wait about 30 minutes to glaze.
7.) GLAZE: combine all ingredients. Pour on glaze.

NOTES:
- These freeze well but are best thawed at room temperature, NOT the microwave.
- These are pictured with mixed berries: ½ cup raspberries, ½ cup blueberries, ½ cup strawberries, ½ cup blackberries.

Breakfast Fusions

This looks like a lot of ingredients, but seriously, this is: dump in and stir! Like 5 minutes, and bake while you're cleaning up supper. It's breakfast on the go, breakfast for little people, coffee snack for moms, lunchbox energy-food for dads, and wholesome food for those boys who are always hungry. These are 183 calories and 11g. of protein each.

Heat oven 350°, Bake 16-18 minutes	Makes 20

Ingredients:

1 ripe banana (small or ½ large)
2 eggs
1/2 cup brown sugar
1 TBSP vanilla
¼ cup butter
1 cup coconut
3 cups oatmeal
1 cup protein powder (unflavored)
1 cup almond flour
½ tsp salt
2 cups chocolate chips

1.) Heat oven.
2.) Place all ingredients in mixer and beat for one minute.
3.) You can mix by hand if you want an arm workout.
4.) Line baking sheet with parchment paper = No cleanup.
5.) I scoop with the biggest cookie scoop.
6.) Bake all 20 on one sheet. They don't spread.

NOTES:

- I use regular sweetened coconut, unsweetened protein powder, and semisweet chocolate chips. If using vanilla protein or milk chocolate you may need to decrease brown sugar.
- They freeze wonderfully! I have my 10-year-old make them.
- If not using protein powder, double the almond flour.
- Yes, there is no leavening. That is not a mistake.
- Don't use too much banana, it can be overpowering.

"Accept who you are in the moment, but acknowledge who you want to become" _Unknown

BROWN SUGAR-VANILLA COFFEE SYRUP:

2 cups brown sugar   1 TBSP vanilla
1 cup water   Pinch of salt

Bring brown sugar and water to a boil. Boil 3 minutes. Remove from heat. Stir in vanilla and salt. Let cool at least one hour before pouring into jars. Hot jars break very easily. Add 1 or 2 TBSP per 16 oz. latte.

BEAUTY MEANS "AN ASSEMBLAGE OF GRACES". _WEBSTER 1828

She was beautiful,
for the kindness in her voice,
the gentleness in her touch,
patience for spilled milk,
encouragement over homework,
her optimism through hard times,
and the sparkle in her eyes to join adventure.
With her willing spirit,
God uses her to minister where no one sees.
His light is woven in her heart,
and her beauty is deeply rooted
in His love. _AAT

"His light was woven in her heart, and His love ran wild in her soul."

Vegetables/Sides
Seven days of salads and our family favorite sides.

Contents:

Chicken BLT Wedge 62

Asian Crunch 65

Special Kale Salad 66

Honey Balsamic w/ Parmesan Crisps 69

Homemade Caesar w/ Rosemary Croutons 70

Olive Garden from Scratch 72

Mo's Salad 75

Old Saylor's Veggie Dip 77

Roasted Carrots 78

Mom's Jello Salad 81

Cheese Dunkers 83

Heidi's Bread 84

Crescent Rolls 87

Perfect Mashed Potatoes 88

Best Oven Fries 91

Chicken BLT Wedge

This is my favorite entrée salad. It's got it all: flavor, crunch, good protein. If you say, "BLT" then the guys will eat it too!! The chicken is a little time consuming, but this may become your new favorite chicken recipe without the salad. Sometimes when I get a little ache inside because life can quickly be very dull, I clean up the kitchen, pour some Diet Coke over ice and start chopping and preparing this salad. It satisfies the creativity and the appetite.

Heated frying pan	Serves 6

Make Salad Dressing:
See picture page 63

Salad:
1 head iceburg lettuce
2 Roma tomatoes
1/3 cup blue cheese crumbles
1 lb. bacon (save ¼ c grease)

Chicken:
1-1/2 lb. chicken breast
¼ c bacon grease
Garlic salt
1/3 cup fine Parmesan cheese
1/3 cup chopped fresh parsley

For Cilantro-Lime Ranch see page 118

1.) Cut iceburg lettuce into six pieces. Place in six bowls.
2.) Dice tomatoes. Sprinkle cheese and tomatoes over lettuce.
3.) Fry bacon, reserve ¼ cup bacon grease. Crumble. Add to salads.
4.) Slice chicken breast ¼" thick. Heat skillet with 2 TBSP bacon grease. (If you use a 10" skillet you will fry the chicken in about 3 batches.)
5.) Place single layer of chicken in pan; sprinkle with garlic salt, 1 TBSP of cheese, and 1 TBSP fresh parsley. Turn in 3 minutes.
6.) Sprinkle the second side with the same as step 5. Cook 3 more minutes. Double check for doneness or 160°.
7.) Repeat steps 5 and 6 for remaining chicken.
8.) Chop chicken. Arrange on salad. Drizzle with dressing.

NOTES:
- If bacon grease is disagreeable to you, use 2 TBSP butter for each pan of chicken. This is a little more than you need but it ensures the crispiness.

"A gossip is someone who is the knife if the party." _Morris Bender

"This recipe is light and crisp,
perfect for a lady's lunch or a summer evening.!"
Kaisa Hill – West Richland, Washington

Asian Crunch
with Peanut Thai Dressing

This is one of those beautiful salads where the vitality is contagious. It has a great group of hardy vegetables that keep well and store well. As with all salad, be mindful of how you chop it. Vegetables like cabbages, are very crunchy. Slice them really thin. No one should feel like they completed a big job when their salad is finished. A good salad should leave you energized, inspired, balanced, and satisfied.

No heat necessary	Serves 6

Base Salad:
4 cups shredded cabbage
2 cups shredded spinach
1 cup shredded red cabbage
1 cup shredded carrots
1 red bell pepper
1 bunch green onion
1 (15 oz.) can mandarin oranges (save juice)
1 cup tortilla strips

Dressing:
Juice from mandarin oranges
¼ cup teriyaki sauce
1/3 cup smooth peanut butter
½ tsp garlic powder
½ tsp ground ginger
1 TBSP rice vinegar
½ cup olive oil

1.) Shave cabbage with sharp knife or buy coleslaw mix. Shred spinach and toss together in serving dish.
2.) Finely slice red cabbage, carrots, and bell pepper. Arrange over base salad. Use a mandolin slicer if you have one.
3.) Garnish with chopped green onion, mandarins (drain juice into blender), and tortilla strips.
4.) DRESSING: Make dressing in blender. Add all ingredients to mandarin juice. Blend 1 minute on high. Dressing will be smooth and fluffy. Store leftovers in fridge.
5.) Serve dressing on the side.
6.) Enjoy! I love this salad.

NOTES:
- Leftover dressing stores well in fridge.
- This is really good as a complete meal with steak, chicken, or shrimp.
- If there are peanut allergies in your house; this is just as good with almond butter.

"Let my words, like vegetables, be tender and sweet, for tomorrow I may have to eat them." _Unknown

Special Kale Salad

Let me tell you what "special" means. Kale is a superfood and we should all eat it, but….. it's really tough! So, here is an amazing technique that changes that. After your kale is washed and chopped, sprinkle it with oil and massage it! Yes, I spelled it right and you read it right. Wash your hands and massage it. It is wonderful!!!

Heat - None	Serves 6

Salad Dressing:

1 large bunch kale (like a bunch that's too big for the bag)
¼ cup olive oil
½ tsp salt
½ tsp pepper
2 tsp sugar
½ fresh lemon

1 cup craisins
1 cup crumbled cheese
(I use goat cheese)
1 cup slivered almonds

1.) Wash kale really well and tear out stems thicker than ¼".
2.) Chop in small pieces. Place in large bowl and drizzle with oil.
3.) Wash your hands. Grab the kale and squish in your hands. Squish about 1 minute. You will see the kale turn bright green as the fibers break open.
4.) Sprinkle with salt, pepper, and sugar. Drizzle with lemon. Toss.
5.) Garnish with craisins, cheese crumbles, and almonds.

Notes:

- I like goat cheese, but that gives some people nightmares. I have used Feta and I have used blue cheese; both are good. Use what your family likes.
- Don't make ahead. If you need to have ready in advance, just wash and prep kale.

About 20 years ago, I went to an open house for someone my husband built a house for. This lady was the most confident cook I had ever met. The way she made salad changed my life. She took a 2 ft. wooden bowl with fresh greens and just started tossing oil, herbs, lemon, salt….. It was a work of art and the best fresh salad I have ever eaten.

"I grated my own parmesan, and the cheese crisps were great.!"
"The girls asked me to test a recipe, and I made almost the whole chapter. Everything was wonderful. I couldn't decide which I should review on."
Diane Matson – Washington State

Honey Balsamic
over Tossed Greens with Parmesan Crisps

This is best described as, "my favorite dinner salad". The spring greens are tender and the dressing is light. There is something in the sweet and tangy that is so satisfying. With every good salad there is something that makes a crunch. The parmesan crisps are super easy, fast, and beautiful, Yep, "beautiful" food can be just lovely.

Heat – oven 400° 4-5 Minutes	Serves 6

SALAD:
10 oz. pkg. spring mix or fresh tossed greens

DRESSING:
¼ cup olive oil
2 TBSP balsamic vinegar
¼ cup honey
¼ tsp salt
¼ tsp coarse pepper

PARMESAN CRISPS:
3/4 cup parmesan cheese
(this needs to be the grated kind)
Sprinkle of dried basil

1.) Wash or prepare greens and place on large flat serving dish.
2.) Mix all dressing ingredients in a small jar and shake.
3.) I drizzle with desired amount of dressing and serve already tossed. If you are unsure of how much salad you need, you can serve the dressing on the side. Once the dressing is on the greens, they only last an hour. Leftovers are discarded.
4.) PARMESAN CRISPS: Heat oven. Line pan with parchment paper. Scoop 1 TBSP of cheese in a pile and spread around slightly. Repeat 12 times. Sprinkle basil.
5.) Bake 4-5 minutes or until golden brown. Cool. Garnish your salad.

NOTES:
- Be a salad artist and put new meaning to the word. Greens are the healthiest thing you can eat and the least expensive vegetable.
- When using this salad as an entrée, I make the "Grilled Chicken" thighs from cookbook #1 page 96.

"The only bar I go to is the salad bar." _On a restaurant wall

Homemade Caesar
with Rosemary Croutons

This is our go-to queen of salads. It's always a crowd pleaser and this is what I usually make if bringing a meal to someone. The homemade dressing takes Caesar to a whole new level. Also, if you are new to making your own croutons, you will be pleasantly surprised how quick and easy they are to make. They make your house smell absolutely wonderful.

Heat 350° 5-7 minutes	Serves 6

SALAD:
- 1 large or 2 small heads of romaine lettuce
- 1 cup grated parmesan cheese

DRESSING:
- 1 cup mayonnaise
- 1 TBSP lemon juice
- 1-1/2 tsp Worcestershire sauce
- 1-1/2 tsp Dijon mustard
- ½ tsp garlic powder
- ½ cup fine parmesan cheese
- 2-1/2 TBSP cold water
- ½ tsp salt
- 2 tsp *coarse ground pepper

CROUTONS:
- 4 croissants
- Butter
- 1 TBSP parmesan cheese
- 1 tsp rosemary

1.) Always wash romaine lettuce no matter what. Cut or tear into 1" pieces. This can be done one day ahead. Store in plastic bag.
2.) Mix all dressing ingredients together. Store in airtight container in refrigerator up to one month.
3.) Cut croissants open. Butter both sides and sprinkle with rosemary, garlic salt, and parmesan cheese. Cut in ½" squares. Toss on baking sheet. Bake 5-7 minutes, stirring halfway through.
4.) Combine salad no more than 15 minutes before eating.
5.) Use only as much dressing as desired.

NOTES:
- Day-old croissants work perfect.
- Traditional Caesar dressing is made with anchovies. I have a personal dislike for them. In this recipe the Worcestershire sauce stands in their place.
- To create an entrée just add grilled chicken.
- *If you don't use coarse pepper, only use a ½ tsp fine ground.

"It is not whether God is on our side, but whether we are on His." _Ronald Reagan

Olive Garden Salad
from scratch

Brandon and my boys are obsessed with airplanes. We usually go on a date, where there is some airplane watching to be done. We love to get take-out from the Arden Olive Garden and watch planes from the Lowes parking lot. Olive Garden is just like 'good times – every time'. We love their soup and salad. We have created our own version of their dressing that is much better for you, but still ensures a good time.

Heat - None	Serves 6

Salad:
- 1 head iceberg lettuce
- 2 Roma tomatoes
- ¾ cup pickled pepperoncini
- ½ Red Onion
- ½ (14.5oz) can black olives, drained
- Grated Parmesan cheese
- 4.5 oz package croutons

Dressing:
- ¼ cup olive oil
- ¼ cup mayonnaise
- 1 TBSP white vinegar
- 1 TBSP fresh lemon juice
- 2 tsp sugar
- 1 tsp salt
- ¾ tsp pepper
- ½ tsp Italian seasoning
- ½ tsp garlic powder
- ¼ cup parmesan cheese

1.) Prepare Dressing. Chill.
2.) Chop iceberg lettuce.
3.) Cut Roma tomatoes in half and slice ¼".
4.) I leave pepperoncini's whole.
5.) Cut red onion as thin as you can.
6.) I leave drained olives whole.
7.) Do not add parmesan or croutons until you are ready to serve.
8.) 15 minutes before eating add desired amount of dressing, croutons, and parmesan.
9.) Toss and serve.

NOTES
- We use croutons from the Ceasar salad recipe page 70.

"Keep your face toward the sunshine and the shadows will fall behind you." Walt Whitham

Mo's Salad
Just the Best

There is this restaurant on the Oregon coast called Mo's Seafood and Chowder. It's still there, but I'm not. In fact, I have not been back to Tolovana Beach since our 5th wedding anniversary, but we went there as kids and we went a lot. This was the salad that I always remember my parents getting. We recreate it now 3,000 miles away and the vibe is still a beach day and good times.

Heat - None	Serves 6

Salad:
1 head iceburg lettuce
1 carrot
Red cabbage if desired
1 lb. pre-cooked shrimp
(these are called salad shrimp or tiny shrimp)
1 bag oyster crackers

Dressing:
1 cup mayo
½ cup ketchup
¼ cup sweet pickle relish
1 hard-boiled egg, chopped
½ tsp salt
¼ tsp pepper

1.) Chop iceburg lettuce. Grate carrot and red cabbage. Toss in large bowl.
2.) Prepare dressing. Yes, you need a hard-boiled egg. Combine all ingredients.
3.) For shrimp: Buy precooked, tiny shrimp. Thaw in cold water. Drain. Press water out with paper towel so they are dry. Sprinkle with salt and pepper. Keep chilled till ready to serve.
4.) Build salads like this:
    a. Lettuce
    b. Shrimp
    c. Dressing
    d. Crackers
5.) We like our crackers crushed.

NOTES:
- This dressing recipe is 100% my mom's!!!! She is a wonderful cook. Yes, that's where we get our cooking skills from. We are using it here with her permission.
- On the left is a lovely picture of mom and us. This picture represents four generations.

"Keep it shrimple" _Unknown

Old Saylor's Veggie Dip

This recipe is just begging me to tell its story. This recipe is mostly about 'home' and 'good memories' and, of course, 'good food'. There is this restaurant in Portland called The Old Country Kitchen. It is like the only restaurant my parents went to when we were growing up. If they were going to "Old Saylor's" it was hot. Now we all live 3,000 miles away and we still go eat there when we vacation, but that's not very often, and with the size of our family it costs an airline ticket or two. So! In my opinion, the dip is the best part. It's time to re-create the dip.

Heat - None	Makes a pint

Dip:

1 cup sour cream
(buy a good brand)
1 cup mayonnaise
(Hellman's or Duke brand)
½ tsp garlic powder
1 TBSP dried chives
½ tsp salt
1 tsp sugar

1.) Mix all ingredients together and chill. I sprinkle a few additional chives on top.
2.) Store in airtight container in the refrigerator, up to one month.
3.) Serve with your choice of vegetables.

NOTES:
- This is the absolute best baked potato topping there is!!!

"That would be cool if you could eat a good food with a bad food and the good food would cover for the bad food when it got to your stomach. Like you could eat a carrot with an onion ring, and they would travel down to your stomach, then they would get there, and the carrot would say, It's cool, he's with me." MITCH HEDBURG

Roasted Carrots

I love vegetables and I really think that is only possible if you have some great recipes. Flavor and texture play a huge part in what a vegetable tastes like. Here is a quick timeless side that is inexpensive, healthy, beautiful, and doesn't fail. I like to roast the carrots peeled and whole. You can also get adventurous and change up the seasoning.

Heat oven 425° - 35-45 minutes	Serves 6

Ingredients:

2 lb. whole carrots
2 TBSP olive oil
½ tsp salt
¼ tsp pepper
4 TBSP brown sugar
Dash cayenne pepper

Garnish with fresh or dried parsley.

1.) Wash carrots, peel if desired.
2.) If carrots are larger than ½" thick at any end, cut in halves and quarters.
3.) Spray cookie sheet with non-stick cooking spray. Toss carrots with oil, salt, peppers, and brown sugar. Spread single layer.
4.) Roast carrots till caramelized, or until fork tender. Toss carrots halfway through cooking.
5.) Heirloom carrots roast as quick as 25 minutes, while more dense regular store carrots take up to 45 minutes.
6.) Sprinkle with fresh herbs right before serving.

NOTES:

- May cook on parchment paper for easy cleanup.
- Leftovers reheat well.
- May cut up carrots and store in plastic the day before.

"Vegetables are a must on a diet. I suggest carrot cake, zucchini bread, and pumpkin pie." _Jim Davis

Raspberry Mom's Jello Salad
Better than Good

My earliest memories are waking up in the morning, and hearing my mom start her baking day. Dishes and pans rattling, the mixer running, yes, we have generations of good cooking. Mom was always cooking for large groups and she made everything from scratch. This jello recipe is one of my favorites she created. My mom gives her permission to share it with our 'cookbook family'. This is super tried and true.

Stovetop - saucepan	Serves 6-8

Ingredients:

- 3 cups cold water
- ½ cup sugar
- 3 TBSP cornstarch
- 1 (3 oz.) box of raspberry Jello
- 3 TBSP Minute tapioca
- 3/4 tsp salt
- 1 TBSP vanilla

- 2 cups whipped cream
- ½ cup powdered sugar
- (or 1 (8oz.) tub Cool whip)
- 2 cups frozen raspberries

1.) In medium saucepan, mix cold water, sugar, cornstarch, Jello, tapioca, salt (measure salt exactly), and vanilla.
2.) While stirring, bring to a boil. Boil for 2 minutes.
3.) Cool for at least 1 hour before adding whipped cream and berries.
4.) For whipped cream: whip cream with powdered sugar till stiff.
5.) Fold into Jello with berries. Do not stir too much, it is pretty to leave streaks of white cream and berries.
6.) Chill completely before serving.

NOTES:

- If making this Jello the day before, I don't add the fruit or whip cream till the day I serve it.
- You can use variations of strawberry Jello and fresh strawberries or orange Jello and canned (drained) mandarin oranges. All are our favorites. If color coordinating a meal you can mix blackberry and strawberry Jello to make purple.:)
- If you buy Jello in bulk use 1/3 cup for 3oz.

"People will forget what you said, they will forget what you did, but they will never forget how you made them feel." _Maya Angelou

Honey Butter

½ cup butter (room temperature)
¼ cup honey
½ tsp cinnamon
Pinch of salt

Whip all ingredients.
Store in an airtight container.

Cheese Dunkers
& Honey Butter

Somewhere between chewy and flaky, these little dunkers are about the ultimate comfort food. They remind you of a corn muffin without the cornmeal. They have a sweet and salty flare that makes them a perfect pair for a great BBQ affair.
Also, use them as appetizers, with brunches, with soup, or any meal combination.
I rate these on the super easy category to make.

Heat oven to 375° - Bake 17 minutes	Yields 12 muffins.

Dry Ingredients:
- 1-1/2 cups flour
- 2/3 cup sugar
- 1 tsp baking powder
- ½ tsp soda
- ½ tsp salt

Wet Ingredients:
- 2 eggs
- 2/3 cup of milk
- 4 TBSP melted butter
- 1 tsp vanilla
- 1 cup shredded cheddar cheese

1.) Preheat oven.
2.) Spray muffin tin, set aside.
3.) In medium mixing bowl, place dry ingredients and whisk.
4.) Add all wet ingredients to dry mixture and stir. This is a one bowl and one spatula, no mess, deal.
5.) Divide batter into muffin tin.
6.) Bake 17 minutes, or until center doesn't poke in when touched.

NOTES:
These can be made ahead of time and frozen.
You can also just make the dough, place in muffin tins, and place in the refrigerator. Bake when you need them. I like to whip them up Sunday morning (takes less than 5 minutes) put my meat baking while we are gone to church and then put the dunkers in the hot oven when I get home. They are fresh and hot by the time the meal is ready.

"Muffins are the language of love, spoken with butter and warmth." _Unknown

Heidi's Bread

I HAVE THIS SUPER SWEET SISTER WHO HAS BROUGHT MORE PEOPLE MEALS THAN I CAN COUNT. SHE IS FAMOUS FOR BRINGING A BATCH OF HER BREAD WITH THOSE MEALS. MANY OF YOU HAVE ASKED FOR THIS RECIPE. I HAVE TRIED TO DESCRIBE HER TECHNIQUES, TO ENSURE YOUR BAKING SUCCESS. BREAD BAKING IS AN ACCOMPLISHMENT. THERE IS NOTHING LIKE COMING HOME TO A HOUSE THAT SMELLS LIKE FRESH BREAD.

Bake 350°/37 minutes/middle rack	Makes 2 loaves

Mixer Bowl:
3 cups very warm water (120°-130°F)
1/3 cup honey
2 TBSP instant yeast

Add:
1-1/2 TBSP salt
¼ cup olive oil
1-1/2 cups whole wheat flour
1-1/2 cups whole oats

Add:
5-6 cups white flour

Note: this dough is very sticky. <u>You must follow directions exactly or dough will be too sticky.</u>

1.) Place very warm water in mixing bowl. Add honey. Stir with whisk. Add yeast and stir. Let proof (means rise) 6-8 minutes.
2.) Add salt, oil, whole wheat flour, and oats. Stir and let rest for 5 minutes.
3.) Using dough hook add 1 cup white flour and let the mixer knead 2 minutes.
4.) Repeat step (3) four more times.
5.) Turn dough onto a sprayed cutting board and divide in half.
6.) Spray 2 metal bread pans.
7.) Shape each dough into a loaf by pressing each piece with the tips of your fingers to work out the air bubbles. Keep folding in the sides to form rectangular loaf.
8.) Place loaf upside down in pan to get a little grease on top. Flip over and poke 15 holes with a fork to work out air.

BAKING INSTRUCTIONS:

- Let loaves rise till they reach the top of pan before baking.
- If your house is cold, raise loaves in 200° oven.
- Use recommended baking time as a guideline. Every oven is different. Loaves are done when golden brown and sound hollow when tapped.
- Remove from oven. Invert onto cooling rack. Butter tops generously while hot. Bag one hour after baking.

Crescent Rolls

I think of crescent rolls as "the life of the party"; that made me think of the following quote: "Life is kind of like a party. You invite a lot of people, some come early, some stay all night, some laugh with you, some laugh at you, and some show up late. But in the end, after the fun, there are a few who stay and help you clean up the mess. And most of the time, they are not even the ones who made it. These people are your real friends. These people matter." _Prince E.A.

Heat 400° - 16-17 minutes	Makes 2 Dozen

Dough:

1 cup whole milk
½ cup butter (1 stick)

¼ cup sugar
1 TBSP instant yeast
2 eggs

4-1/2 cups flour
2 tsps salt

4 TBSP butter (after it's rolled out, 2 TBSP on each)
Butter for tops, after baked

1.) In microwave safe bowl heat milk and butter (slice up butter, melts better). Heat 2-1/2 minutes.
2.) Add sugar, yeast, and eggs to milk and whisk altogether.
3.) In stand mixer place flour and salt. Whisk. Make a dip in the flour and pour the wet ingredients into your dip. Stir with a spoon until a lumpy dough forms.
4.) Place dough hook on mixer and let knead for 5 minutes. Cover mixing bowl, let dough rise in 200° oven for at least 30 minutes.
5.) When dough is doubled, dump onto a greased cutting board. Cut in 2 pieces.
6.) On cutting board roll each dough into a 16" circle. Butter with 2 TBSP butter. Cut in 12 pieces.
7.) Roll from the outside in. Place on greased baking sheet. Tip down.
8.) Let rise on pan another 30 minutes.
9.) Bake till golden brown. Remove from oven, lightly butter tops.

Super Easy Recipe
Cut Pattern↓

- If you don't like microwaves, use a pot on the stove. Don't overheat the milk, or it will burn your yeast.
- I bake on parchment. I fit all 2 dozen on one cookie sheet.

Perfect Mashed Potatoes

There is really nothing romantic to say about mashed potatoes. On the flip side, when dried out mashed potatoes start to act like oatmeal on your spoon, they become very unromantic. I don't like the flavor of sour cream or cream cheese in my potatoes unless it's a baked potato casserole, so here are my little secrets for great mashed potatoes.

Heat oven 350° - 40 minutes - Covered	Serves 12 adults – Makes 9x13

Ingredients:
5# Russet potatoes

2 tsp salt

1 tsp coarse pepper

½ cup butter

1 cup milk

Garnish:
Butter
Paprika
Parsley

1.) Wash and peel.
2.) Cut 1" cubes. Rinse.
3.) Cover with cold water (If you want them to sit up to 4 hours). Cover with hot water if you want them done right away.
4.) Bring to a boil. Boil 10 minutes or until fork tender. Drain.
5.) Add salt, pepper, and butter. Beat out lumps for two minutes. (you have to do this before you add the milk)
6.) Add milk, beat 1 more minute.
7.) Spread in pan or serving dish.
8.) Garnish right before you serve.

NOTES:
- Potatoes absorb moisture. If making potatoes more than 2 hours before eating them, add an extra ½ cup of milk. They will be almost soupy when you mix them, and they will be perfect when you serve them.
- If freezing mashed potatoes, cover with plastic wrap then foil.
- When thawing, take out of freezer in the morning and let sit on the counter till baking at supper. Remove plastic. Replace foil. Bake 350° for 40 minutes.
- If 5# is too much for your family, freeze an 8x8. You will love having this side already made. Mashed potatoes are a lot of dishes.

"Being a king, emperor, or president is mighty small potatoes compared to being a mother." _Billy Sunday

Best Oven Fries

In the age of air fryers and such, maybe this recipe is outdated?! Needless to say, I still make these like once a week, and that's pretty much a staple. The kids love them, Dad loves them, you can add different seasonings and different dipping sauces. They are healthy and budget friendly. I usually put these cooking in the oven and put my meat on the grill. While both are cooking, I make a nice salad or veggie tray.

Heat oven 450° Uncovered – 40 minutes	Serves 4-6

Ingredients:

- 2-3 lb. of Russet potatoes (this is about 4 large)
- 3 TBSP oil
- 1 tsp. salt
- 2 TBSP parmesan cheese (powdered kind)

1.) Heat Oven.
2.) Spray cookie sheet, or line with foil and spray that. No cleanup.
3.) Wash and dry potatoes.
4.) Cut into ¼ - ½ inch fry shaped pieces. Do NOT wash.
5.) Pile on cookie sheet. Drizzle with oil and toss to coat.
6.) Bake 20 minutes and stir. Bake 15 minutes and add parmesan cheese and salt. Bake 5 more minutes.
7.) Serve immediately.

NOTES:

- The baking instructions are for room temperature potatoes. Refrigerated potatoes may take another 5 minutes.
- Do not wash. This helps them get crispy. Don't overload the pan or they won't get as crispy.
- Do not salt until they are cooked. The salt pulls the water out and they won't get as crispy.
- Parmesan cheese is optional.
- If you like truffle fries, just substitute for truffle oil and away you go. Sprinkle with ½ tsp basil before serving.
- I buy Red Robin seasoning from Red Robin. That's a favorite too.
- Chop up leftovers for breakfast "home-fries".

"We are a few French fries short of a happy meal around here." _Unknown

Cultivate Your Home

"CULTIVATE" TO IMPROVE BY LABOR OR STUDY, TO REFINE, TO CHERISH, TO PROMOTE INCREASE, TO IMPROVE BY CORRECTION OF FAULTS. _ WEBSTER 1828 DICTIONARY

"Less House, More Home."

Simple Decorations and furniture that lets you spend less time cleaning and organizing. "A place for everything and everything in its place."

Choose durable fabrics or leathers that are easy to clean and can tolerate rough movement of pets or children. Say, "NO" to carpet if possible.

Keep a well-stocked kitchen to put together quick and healthy meals. Hang a meal-plan chalkboard on the wall and fill it out every week.

Decorate with heirlooms. Use your grandma's China and tell stories about her when you use them. It's ok if it doesn't match your décor.

Have a modest home so you have money to travel and keep your horizons big. Also, invest in good books and educational games.

Create deep rest with uncluttered bedrooms. Invest in good mattresses, soft bedding and blankets with calming textures.

Embrace each season. Refresh simple décor and box up items for storage that won't be needed till next year. (beach towels/winter jackets) I keep two seasonal items in each room.

Adjust the mood of your home with lamps and soft lighting, music, plants, throw blankets, and candles. Focus on warmth and welcome.

"The strength of a nation derives from the integrity of the home" _Confucius

Sauces, Rubs & Marinades

"A good spice often deceives us into thinking someone is a good cook." _Mokokoma

Contents:

- Tartar Sauce 96
- Japanese Steakhouse white sauce 96
- Korean BBQ Sauce 97
- North Carolina BBQ Sauce 97

- Rub 101 98
- Rub for the Birds 98
- Rub for the Pig 99
- Rub for the Beef 99

- Topping Off Marinade 100
- Hot Honey BBQ 100
- Southern Teriyaki Glaze 101
- Chicken Citrus Soak 101

FAVORITE SAUCES

TARTAR SAUCE

Ingredients:
¾ cup mayonnaise
1 TBSP dill relish
1-1/2 tsp parsley flakes
1-1/2 tsp minced onion
1/8 tsp salt
1/8 tsp pepper

Directions:
Combine all ingredients, and blend well. Cover and refrigerate until ready to serve.

Makes 1 cup
Stores up to one month.

This sauce is used for seafood dishes, and at our house we make a 'quick meal' with fish-sticks, homemade fries, and tartar sauce.

Note:
Why so many sauces? Well, any sauce homemade is healthier than store bought. If you purchase the healthier version of sauces from the store, they're not very affordable. All our sauces can be made with olive oil, avocado mayo, and cane sugar or honey. The most important is- NO preservatives.

JAPANESE STEAKHOUSE WHITE SAUCE

Ingredients:
1-1/2 cups mayonnaise
¼ cup water
1 TBSP ketchup
1 TBSP melted butter
½ tsp garlic powder
1 tsp sugar
¼ tsp paprika
Dash of cayenne pepper

Directions:
Whisk all ingredients together. Store in a sealed container, up to one month. It's best when it sits overnight, so I usually double this batch, so I have lots of leftovers.

I strongly recommend Hellmann's mayonnaise; also, it is called "Best Foods" west of the Rockies.

This is that wonderful sauce they serve you at hibachi restaurants. My kids won't eat rice without it. It rounds out any stir-fry dish.

It is also known as, "Shrimp Sauce." (that is only because of the color)
If you buy it in the store it is called "Yum-Yum Sauce."

WITH HEART

KOREAN BBQ

INGREDIENTS:
1 ripe pear
1 cup cold water
½ cup soy sauce
1 TBSP minced garlic
½ cup brown sugar
2 TBSP rice vinegar
2 TBSP apple cider vinegar
2 TBSP olive oil
½ tsp. ground ginger
2 TBSP corn starch
1 tsp salt

DIRECTIONS:
Peel pear and cut out seeds. Place pear and water in blender. Add blended pear and all other ingredients to a small saucepan. Bring to a boil for 1 minute.

Cool before placing in an airtight jar. Store in refrigerator 1 month.

We love this sauce for stir-fry, meatballs, burgers, chicken marinade, and Ramen Bowl drizzle.

NC BBQ SAUCE

INGREDIENTS:
2 cups ketchup
1/3 cup bacon grease
½ cup brown sugar
1/3 cup water
1/3 cup apple cider vinegar
1 TBSP Worcestershire sauce
1 tsp paprika
1 tsp. coarse pepper
1 tsp cumin
1 tsp salt

DIRECTIONS:
Place all ingredients in a small saucepan and bring to a boil. You can reduce heat immediately. Simmer 5 minutes.

Cool before placing in an airtight jar. Store in refrigerator 1 month.

This is my go-to BBQ sauce! Think: pulled-pork, ribs, grilled chicken…..

At my house we call this "Brisket Sauce" We changed the name for this book so no one would think it's only for brisket, but I will add, we have traveled from Texas to Tennessee, and I have rarely found anything this good.

"A nation has begun to get back on its feet, when it gets down on its knees." Unknown

BASIC DRY RUBS

RUB 101

INGREDIENTS:
2 TBSP coarse black pepper
2 TBSP kosher salt
2 TBSP garlic powder

DIRECTIONS:
Stir all ingredients together. Store in an airtight container.

This is basic, but less is more.
I use this rub for:

Pot roast
Oven roast
Prime rib
Pork shoulder
Brisket
Ribs
Pork Tenderloin

RUB FOR THE BIRDS

INGREDIENTS:
2 tsp garlic powder
1 tsp onion powder
1 tsp thyme
1 tsp sage
1 TBSP sugar
1 tsp salt
2 tsp bouillon

DIRECTIONS:
Stir all ingredients together. Store in an airtight container.

For marinating chicken: Rinse, pat dry, coat with olive oil, and toss with rub. This is enough for 2 lb. of chicken.

For roasting chicken: Rinse, pat dry, rub with oil and seasoning. Sprinkle some seasoning inside the cavity of the bird.

THE ART OF SPICES.
On Amazon you can find cute matching inexpensive jars and labels. Spices are beautiful to display, even in a cupboard. This brings inspiration into cooking.

THE GIFT OF SPICES.
Mix up some extra batches of rub, package it cute!
If you know a guy that grills or cooks, this is the perfect gift.
You have my permission to bottle it and sell it. Do a craft fair!

FOR THE MEAT

RUB FOR THE PIG

INGREDIENTS:
2 TBSP brown sugar
2 tsp coarse salt
1 tsp coarse pepper
1 tsp paprika
1/8 tsp cayenne pepper
½ tsp ground mustard
1 tsp garlic powder

DIRECTIONS:
Stir all ingredients together. Store in an airtight container.

This is the basic rub I use for pulled pork and smoked pork.

See pork recipes for liquid basting options. Save a little of this seasoning to sprinkle over meat after it's pulled apart.

RUB FOR THE BEEF

INGREDIENTS:
1 TBSP paprika
1 TBSP garlic powder
1 TBSP onion powder
1 TBSP salt
1 TBSP cumin
1 TBSP black pepper

DIRECTIONS:
Stir all ingredients together. Store in an airtight container.

You can make this and keep on hand for burgers, short ribs, ground beef, etc. See "Taco Cups" for taco seasoning.

There is nothing as welcoming as the smell of well-seasoned meat cooking.

NOTE: Stock your spice cupboard! You can go to a spice shop and have a really fun time sniffing and filling all the little baggies, but then you should really put them in jars. Most of the time I get on my Walmart app and order up whatever I'm out of. (Walmart is at least 50% cheaper than anywhere else, and they sell their own brand for pennies.) I quit buying most of my spices at big box stores because they get old before I use them, and they don't fit in my matching jar system.

HISTORY:

It's fun to stop and think that there was a time when spices reshaped the world. Even Christopher Columbus founded our country seeking gold and spices. I can't write a history book on spices, but let's take 5 seconds and think:
ANCIENT • FLAVOR • CALMING • DIGESTION • PRESERVING • MEDICINE.

FLAVOR BURSTING

TOPPING OFF MARINADE

THINK steak!

INGREDIENTS:
1 cup A-1 sauce
¼ cup Worcestershire
½ cup BBQ sauce
1/3 cup minced garlic
¼ cup soy sauce
¼ cup apple cider vinegar
1 cup brown sugar

DIRECTIONS:
Mix all ingredients in a bowl and you are ready to go! Place meat in Ziplock bag, cover with marinade, let sit in refrigerator 2 hours up to 24 hours. Turn bag over at least once halfway through marinating.
(I figure 1 cup marinade to 2lb. meat, this fits nicely in a gallon Ziplock).

HOT HONEY BBQ

THINK chicken!

INGREDIENTS:
¾ cup ketchup
½ cup honey
1 TBSP cider vinegar
1 TBSP Worcestershire
1 TBSP Dijon mustard
¼ tsp cumin
½ tsp garlic powder
¼ tsp of cayenne

DIRECTIONS:
Mix all ingredients in a small pan and simmer 3 minutes. Cool slightly. Divide sauce in half. Marinate in one half and pour the other half over meat right before you serve.

Use 2lb. of chicken. Marinate 2 hours, up to 24 hours. Grill over medium heat or 160° inside temp.

JUST FOR FUN! The "Topping Off Marinade" was born when Dave worked for Ace/Avant. After pushing his crew to hit a tight schedule, he felt the morale of the job was down. He brought three grills to the job and had a fiesta. We bought (5) 20# rib roasts and hand carved them into steaks. Dave made up the marinade from what I had in the house. The next job the guys asked him to do it again and "please make the same meat." On about the third or fourth cookout, I finally wrote down a recipe.

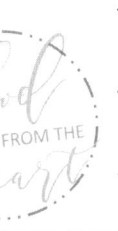

FUN MARINADES

SOUTHERN TERIYAKI GLAZE

THINK fish

INGREDIENTS:
1/3 cup olive oil
1/3 cup soy sauce
¼ cup brown sugar
2 TBSP minced garlic
1 tsp ginger powder
1 squeezed lime
1 TBSP sriracha

DIRECTIONS:
Whisk all ingredients together in a small pot. Bring to a boil. Boil one minute. Cool for a few minutes before pouring over meat. I use this on salmon, tilapia, or chicken. If you like it spicier add more sriracha. For great tilapia, marinade 30 minutes. Grill at 350-400° in a tin foil boat for 10-12 minutes or until fish temperature is 145°. I make a double batch of the sauce and reserve half the sauce to serve over rice.

CHICKEN CITRUS SOAK

THINK Gyros

INGREDIENTS:
Zest of 1 lime
1 TBSP lemon juice
¼ cup oil
¼ cup Greek yogurt
1 tsp minced garlic
1 TBSP fresh dill
½ tsp salt
1 tsp coarse pepper
½ tsp cumin
2 tsp parsley

DIRECTIONS:
Wisk together. Pour in Ziplock bag with 2 lbs. chicken thighs.
Marinate 30 min to 2 hours.

Grill on gas BBQ at medium heat until internal temperature reaches 160°.

This is great chicken for the Gyros on page 157.

DID YOU KNOW? A good marinade can be complex or simple, but you need three basic components: sweet, salt, and acidic. The sugar promotes browning and caramelization, which creates great looks and texture. The salt creates osmosis which pulls the meat juice out but replaces it with marinade flavor. The acid (usually vinegar, wine or citrus) works as a tenderizer. So, be free to make up your own!

motherhood

"Motherhood is amazing,

then it is really hard,

then it is incredible,

then it is everything in-between.

So, hold onto the good,

breathe through the bad,

Cherish the moments,

and pray through it all."

_AAT

FIESTA CON AMIGOS
"Party with Friends"

Contents:

Chicken Tacos	107
Steak Tacos	108
Shrimp Tacos	111
Carnitas	112
Homemade Queso	115
Homemade Guacamole	116
Chicken Taquitos	119
Taco Bowls	120
Beef Enchiladas	123
Chicken Enchiladas	124

DEFINED: "Fiesta" refers to a large feast, festival, or party. ● Derived from the Latin word "festus" ● festive, joyful, or merry. "Amigo" ● friend.

Pickled Onions

1 large red onion
2 cups hot water
1-1/2 cups white vinegar
½ tsp salt
2 cloves fresh garlic
¼ tsp crushed red pepper
3 TBSP sugar

Slice onions the opposite of circles, (North to South Pole).
Place all ingredients in quart jar.

CHICKEN TACOS

I'm not a big fan of onions but there is something about these pickled onions that you have got to try (recipe on page 106). Trust me, they are more than pretty. Make a jar and keep them on hand in the frig. If you want to add this meal to your list of pantry/freezer meals, buy the precut onion and pepper mix from the freezer section, and always cook extra chicken. It is the most efficient leftover in your frig.

Heat skillet	Serves 4-6

Ingredients:

3 cups cooked chopped chicken
2 TBSP taco seasoning
¼ cup water

1 TBSP olive oil
1 green pepper
1 red pepper
1 small onion
½ tsp garlic salt

12 corn tortillas

Toppings:

Queso Cheese
Cilantro
Pickled or grilled onions
Limes

1.) Chop cooked chicken. Place in hot skillet with taco seasoning and water. Sauté 3 minutes. Place in dish and set aside.

2.) In same skillet heat oil. Sauté peppers, onions, and garlic salt for 5 minutes. Set aside.

3.) Spray or oil skillet and grill tortillas on both sides. This is only enough to heat them and not hardly turn them brown. Stack and wrap in foil to keep warm.

4.) Heat queso. Chop cilantro. Set out pickled onions. Cut limes in wedges.

5.) Build tacos with chicken first, then vegetables, then toppings.

NOTES:

- My Preference is to use leftover grilled chicken or leftover rotisserie chicken.
- You may also use homemade taco seasoning on page 121.
- To reheat frozen corn tortillas: wrap tightly in foil and place in the oven on 350° for 15-20 minutes.

"When the power of love overcomes the love of power, the world will know peace." — Jimi Hendrix

STEAK TACOS

My brother-in-law makes the best steak tacos ever! These tacos are really about the meat. I would call this perfect 'guy' food, but I crave them myself. You can make them with a lesser expensive meat but they're not quite as good. With tacos, a little meat goes a long way. I suggest going to your meat counter and asking them to slice a "beef loin" roast or a "sirloin roast". Have them slice it for you in 1/8" slices. Our Costco has it already sliced.

Heat cast iron skillet/Blackstone grill	Serves 3 people per lb.

Ingredients:
2 lb. thin sliced beef loin roast
½ cup butter
Lawry's seasoning

Corn tortillas
Oil for heating tortillas

Toppings:
Fresh diced raw onion
Or grilled onions
Fresh cilantro
Lime wedges
Salsa verde

1.) Take each 1/8" steak and cut into ½ wide strips (stack up a pile to cut quickly). Set aside.
2.) Heat cast iron pan to high heat. Melt 2 TBSP butter. When bubbly add ½ lb. meat.
3.) Sprinkle generously with Lawry's seasoning.
4.) Stir meat 5-6 minutes or till slightly burned edges. Repeat this step for the rest of the meat.
5.) Heat tortillas in a lightly oil skillet. As they are done, stack in a pot with a lid to keep warm.
6.) Chop topping. We suggest you use all the toppings listed. Absolutely the best.

NOTES:
- Trader Joe's has the best salsa verde for a very reasonable price; when you go there, stock up.
- If you have a Blackstone grill, you can make several batches at a time. If using the Blackstone, use oil instead of butter. Throw a few jalapenos on the grill to soften and slice lengthwise before serving.
- Remember good tacos should be served with ice cold drinks.

"I'm nacho type, don't taco bout love." —AAT

Jalapeno Ranch

½ cup sour cream
1 cup mayonnaise
½ cup milk
¼ cup Jalapeno juice
(from the jar of pickled Jalapenos)
2 TBSP Hidden Valley Ranch mix

½ cup cilantro
1 tsp garlic powder
½ tsp salt
¾ tsp cumin
1 tsp onion powder

Place all ingredients in blender or food processor. Pulse. May turn light green.

SHRIMP TACOS

One of our favorite date spots was Chuy's Mexican restaurant. Brandon would always get the shrimp tacos. Then I tried them and we were both hooked. That was dangerous, so we started making them at home. They just keep getting better. We not only don't order shrimp tacos anymore, we've even forgotten about Chuy's.

Heat Oven 400°	Serves 4-6

Ingredients:
2 lbs. medium size breaded shrimp.
8 flour tortillas 8" size

Fresh Pico:
8 small or 5 large Roma Tomatoes
2/3 cup chopped white onion
3 TBSP chopped green pepper
1/3 cup cilantro
1 clove fresh garlic
2 TBSP fresh lime juice
½ tsp salt

Toppings:
Shaved Red Cabbage
Pickled/grilled onions
Fresh Jalapenos
Lime wedges

Jalapeno Ranch Page 110

1.) Line baking sheet with foil. Bake shrimp according to package directions. While baking….
2.) Make fresh Pico. Chop tomatoes without seeds (see page 116 step 3). Chop and combine all other ingredients. Cover. Set aside.
3.) Mix together Jalapeno ranch. This is a must!!!
4.) Chop cabbage, onions, and jalapenos for toppings.
5.) Flash heat tortillas in a skillet lightly oiled. Stack and wrap with foil.
6.) Tacos must be eaten as assembled.
7.) Assemble with:
    Tortilla
    6 shrimp
    Pico
    Cabbage
    Jalapeno ranch
    Pickled onions
    Fresh Jalapenos

NOTES:
- If you have strong onion. Soak in ice water and 1 TBSP lime juice for 15 minutes before adding to Pico.
- I buy the 1 lb. bags of shrimp from Trader Joe's or the breaded shrimp from Costco. Both are really good.

"Never let success get to your head, and never let failure get to your heart." _Drake

Perfect Pulled Pork
CARNITAS [kär'nēdəz]

GIRLS, YOU NEED TO KNOW HOW TO MAKE THIS. HERE'S WHY: 15 MINUTES OF PREP AND YOU DON'T EVEN NEED TO LIFT THE LID TILL IT'S DONE. THERE ARE SEVERAL AMAZING DISHES TO BE MADE WITH THIS MEAT. IT'S PERFECT FOR ALL FOR SEASONS OF THE YEAR. IT IS A MEAT THAT OFTEN GOES ON SALE. IT IS ONE OF THE MOST ECONOMICAL MEATS TO FEED A CROWD. IT FREEZES PERFECTLY AND CAN BE THAWED QUICKLY.

6 qt. Crock Pot – High for 8-9 hours	Serves 8-10

INGREDIENTS:
8-pound pork butt
(I like bone-in)

RUB:
4 tsp salt
1-1/2 tsp coarse pepper
3 tsp garlic powder
3 tsp ground cumin
1-1/2 TBSP dried oregano

1 small onion, cut in rings
3 jalapenos deseeded and chopped
Juice from 2 oranges

1.) Rinse meat, pat dry with paper towel. Coat with rub *(Reserve 2 TBSP for after cooking)*.
2.) Place in slow cooker with the fat side up.
3.) Top with onions, jalapenos, and orange juice.
4.) Cook in crockpot for 6 hours.
5.) Remove from broth about 15 minutes before you want to serve it *(this helps so you don't burn your hands)*. Pull apart with two forks or your hands. Remove bone and larger pieces of fat.
6.) If using in tacos, spread meat on a baking sheet. Drizzle with about ½ cup of broth from the crockpot and remaining rub. Then place under broiler till the edges are crispy.

NOTES:
FREEZE LEFTOVERS IN MEAL SIZE SERVINGS AND ENJOY ANY OF THE FOLLOWING:

TACOS • BURRITOS • ENCHILADAS • NACHOS • PULLED PORK SANDWICHES • BBQ PORK WITH SIDES • KOREAN BBQ SLIDERS • SHEPHERD'S PIE • BREAKFAST HASH • CHILI • TACO SOUP • STUFFED PEPPERS • EGG ROLLS • PORK ROMAN BOWLS

"My husband's adventures take him far from home. Mine start in the crock pot." _Myself

KNOW YOUR MEAT! Pork shoulder and pork butt are both from the shoulder of the pig. Pork butt is higher on the foreleg and pork shoulder is farther down. Pork butt is fattier, more tender, and more marbled than the shoulder. Both cuts are sold for slow cooking, but the pork butt is definitely best for pulled pork.

The acid in the orange juice works for a tenderizer.

Meat cooked on a bone usually has more flavor. That goes for all meat.

"The Carnitas turns out incredibly tender and full of flavor. The tacos are fabulous to say the least! I highly recommend the homemade Pico and queso to go along with it. This recipe is perfect for an after-church lunch or a party because everything can be prepped in advance!"

Karmyn Karon – Landrum, SC

WHITE QUESO DIP

"Queso" means 'cheese' in Spanish, but it may not be as Mexican as we think. Early American history gives San Antonio, Texas, the credit for queso cheese dip. The way it stands today is; if the queso has a yellow based cheese, it is Texan, if it has a white based cheese, it is Tex-Mex. I just love that bit of history, because San Antonio is one of my favorite cities in America. If you ever get to go there, take a boat tour along the river walk.

Heat on stovetop	Makes 12 (1/4 cup) servings

Ingredients:

½ cup whipping cream
1 cup milk
½ tsp garlic powder
½ tsp onion powder
1 tsp cumin

½ lb. pepper jack cheese
½ lb. white American cheese

½ of (4 oz.) can green chilies

1.) Do not boil or scorch at any time during the process. Do NOT multitask.
2.) In a medium heavy-duty saucepan, place cream, milk, and seasoning.
3.) While this is heating, chop cheese slices into 1" cubes.
4.) When milk is hot, add half the pepper jack cheese and stir till smooth. Repeat with pepper jack, and repeat two times with American cheese.
5.) Stir in green chiles.
6.) Remove from heat.
7.) Serve hot.

NOTES:

- For a non-spicy version, use Monterey Jack cheese.
- Store leftovers in a glass jar. If you reheat in microwave, stir every 30 seconds, uncovered.

"QUESO" Spanish for cheese.
"K, SO:" Southern for, here's the plan and y'all probably aren't going to like it. _Restaurant wall

HOMEMADE GUACAMOLE

If I was really truthful, I would have to say that the best part of Mexican food, for me, is the guacamole and the queso. Guacamole is a Mexican food which dates back to the Aztecs in the 1500's. "Ahuaca-mulli" was a staple food for this tribe as the avocados supply essential nutrients and healthy fats. Our Americanized guacamole has added cilantro and lime to the original dish. Guacamole is healthy and delicious.

Heat-none	Serves 6

Ingredients:

- 3 avocados, peeled and mashed
- ¼ cup white onion, finely chopped
- ½ Roma tomato, seeds out, diced
- 2 TBSP cilantro chopped
- ½ green pepper, finely chopped
- 1 TBSP lime juice
- 1 large clove fresh garlic
- ¾ tsp. salt

1.) To peel an avocado run a knife all the way around the pit, starting at the stem. Twist between your palms and it should pop apart. Take a spoon and remove pit. Now scoop/scrape avocado from its skin. Mash with a fork.
2.) Prepare onion.
3.) Prepare tomato. Hold tomato in your left hand and cut off the outer layer (like you would cut an apple away from the core). Chop these outer pieces for the tomato. This prevents slimy wet tomato juice/seeds.
4.) We use green pepper, if wanting to make spicy guac use jalapenos.
5.) Combine all ingredients and serve.

NOTES:

- Avocados turn brown when the oxygen reaches them. You can prevent this by pressing plastic wrap directly on the guacamole and lightly pressing it down to remove air bubbles. If you do this, you can make up to 2 days ahead or save leftovers.
- Also, you can smooth the guacamole flat and squeeze a lime over it.
- For this reason, traditional Mexicans put the avocado pit in the bowl with the guacamole.

"Don't let anyone treat you like free salsa; you are guacamole. Baby, you are guacamole" _Unknown

Cilantro/Lime Ranch

½ cup sour cream
½ cup milk
½ cup mayonnaise
½ tsp dill
½ tsp garlic powder
½ tsp coarse black pepper
½ tsp salt
Juice of 1 lime
3 TBSP finely chopped fresh cilantro

Mix all ingredients.
Store in an airtight container.

CHICKEN TAQUITOS
with Cilantro Lime Ranch

Quick and Easy ~ Dinner Must be Done

THIS IS IT GIRLS!! DINNER MUST BE DONE! SO WHY NOT HAVE LOTS OF TOOLS IN YOUR TOOLBOX TO WHIP IT UP QUICK, FUN, AND FULL OF FLAVOR. KID FRIENDLY, DAD FRIENDLY, BUDGET FRIENDLY, THAT'S HOW WE LIKE IT. THE CILANTRO LIME RANCH IS FOUND ON PAGE 118. I KNOW THIS IS GOING TO BE ONE OF YOUR NEW FAVORITE GO-TO DINNERS. FOLLOW BAKING INSTRUCTIONS AND TURN HALF-WAY THROUGH BAKING.

Heat oven 425° Bake 22 minutes	Makes 20 - Serves appx. 6

Filling:
- 4 cups of cooked diced chicken
- 4 oz. softened cream cheese
- ½ cup sour cream
- 2 cups grated cheddar cheese
- ¼ cup canned jalapeños, minced
- ¼ cup jalapeno juice

- 20 tortillas 10"

- ½ cup butter
- 2 tsp taco seasoning

Serve with:
- Cilantro Lime Ranch
- Salsa

1.) Line baking sheet with foil. Spray.
2.) Combine all six ingredients of filling. It is fairly stiff. You can use your hands if you want.
3.) Lay out tortillas.
4.) Place ¼ cup of filling on each. Spread filling out in a line the diameter of the tortilla.
5.) Roll and place on baking sheet, with the seam down.
6.) Here's the secret to tight rolling: *<u>Fold the tortilla over till the edge touches the filling. Then roll tight.</u>
7.) Melt butter and stir in taco seasoning. Brush on half of the butter and bake for 12 minutes. <u>Turn each taquito over</u> and baste with remaining butter. Cook appx. 10 more minutes-till crispy.

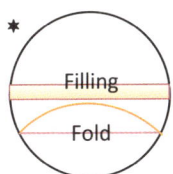

NOTES:
You can make these ahead of time. Do not brush with butter till you are ready to bake. Make Ranch sauce while they bake.

"Don't follow your dreams, chase them!" _Unknown

TACO CUPS

Here is a quick but cute supper that the kids will love! This is also a good supper to let them help you in the kitchen. They really can't mess anything up but the kitchen! Letting kids help cook drives me crazy, but let me tell you, it's a serious investment, they learn fast, and before you know it, they can cook up a whole meal. Embrace these little moments: put some music on, fix both of you a cold drink, and let them do a little tasting too!

Heat oven 400° 5-6 minutes	Serves 6 (2 in a serving)

TACO CUPS:
12 flour tortillas (fajita size)
Olive oil spray
Taco seasoning

MEAT:
1# hamburger
2 TBSP taco seasoning
1 can refried beans
1 cup grated cheddar cheese

TOPPINGS:
Lettuce
Onion
Sour cream
Salsa
Olives
Taco sauce

1.) Chop and prepare all your toppings. Set aside.
2.) Spray tortillas lightly, both sides. Press tightly into muffin tin. Sprinkle each with a small pinch of taco seasoning. Bake till crispy. While baking. Prepare meat.
3.) In skillet, brown hamburger. Drain. Add taco seasoning.
4.) Heat refried beans.
5.) Sprinkle cheese into bottom of hot shell and return to oven till melted.
6.) Scoop beans and meat on top of melted cheese and serve immediately.
7.) I have everyone add their own toppings.
8.) May be eaten with a fork or picked up like a taco.

NOTES:

I only use homemade taco seasoning, but some people think homemade is never as good as boughten, so I wrote this recipe with boughten. If buying I buy McCormick's. On the right is what I use for my family. Now you have the option.

"Cooking with kids is not just about ingredients, recipes, and cooking. It's about harnessing imagination, empowerment, and creativity." – Guy Fieri

Taco Seasoning

1 TBSP chili powder
½ tsp paprika
1-1/2 tsp ground cumin
1 tsp salt
1 tsp pepper
1/8 tsp cayenne pepper
¼ tsp onion powder
¼ tsp garlic powder

Use ¼ cup water.
I use 1 TBSP per lb. of meat.
Yields 2 rounded TBSP.

BEEF ENCHILADAS

This is a quick weeknight supper, and another pantry meal. Take the extra minutes and prepare the meat as instructed below. It's what makes this dish stand out.

Why do we put easy recipes in cookbooks? Well, did you ever have a day that you just wished was over before supper was even started? We have too. Take a minute to go hold your crying baby or send a sweet text to your hubby. You will still have dinner on the table.

Heat oven 375º - 25 minutes - Uncovered	Serves 4-6

Ingredients:
- 1 lb. hamburger
- 1 packet taco seasoning
- 1/3 cup water
- 1 cup Mexican blend grated cheese
- 8 (8") flour tortillas
- 1 (12oz.) can Hatch enchilada sauce, mild
- 1-1/2 cups Mexican blend grated cheese

Garnish:
- Lettuce
- Sour cream
- Tomatoes

1.) Spray 9x13 pan. Spread ¼ cup enchilada red sauce on bottom.
2.) Brown hamburger. Drain. Add seasoning and water. Simmer 5 minutes. This gets the flavor in the meat. Pour meat in food processor or blender. Pulse just enough to make a fine meat.
3.) Fill tortillas with meat mixture, about 1/3 cup each. Then sprinkle 2 TBSP cheese over meat and roll. Place in pan.
4.) Cover with remaining sauce and sprinkle with cheese.
5.) Bake uncovered.
6.) Garnish and serve.

NOTES:
- Hatch enchilada sauce is the best. It's worth the price, you only need one can per recipe. Can be found at Whole Foods, Ingles, and Publix. It makes this a 15-minute prep meal. If you want sauce from scratch, see book one.
- This dish freezes well. Make two and freeze one. Reheat from frozen, covered, 45 minutes, 375º.

"BREATHE, it's just a bad day, not a bad life." _#Motivation

CHICKEN ENCHILADAS

Add this recipe to your list of pantry meals. This is a recipe that you can keep everything on hand in the pantry or freezer. If you keep cooked, canned, or rotisserie chicken on hand, I have put this dish together in 8 minutes. Seriously, make a list of these kind of meals. The next time you are tempted by some expensive, sodium laden takeout, have a backup plan. Take an extra minute to serve a nice drink too. Preferably with lots of ice!

Heat oven 375° - 25minutes - Uncovered	Serves 6

Ingredients:

- 3 cups shredded chicken
- 2 cups Mexican cheese
- 1 (4oz.) can green chilies
- 2/3 cup plain Greek yogurt
- 1 TBSP lime juice
- 1 tsp garlic powder
- ½ tsp cumin
- 1 tsp coarse black pepper
- 2 TBSP honey
- 8 (8") flour tortillas
- 1 (15oz) can green enchilada sauce
- 1 cup Monterey Jack cheese

Toppings:

- Avocado chunks
- Chopped cilantro
- Diced purple onion
- Lime wedges

1.) Make enchilada filling. In medium bowl place shredded chicken, cheese, chilies, yogurt, lime, garlic, cumin, pepper, and honey. Stir to combine.
2.) Spray bottom of 9x13 pan. Spread ¼ cup enchilada sauce on bottom of pan.
3.) Start assembling enchiladas by adding ½ cup of filling to each tortilla. Roll and place in pan.
4.) Drizzle with remaining enchilada sauce.
5.) Sprinkle with cheese.
6.) Cover with foil and bake.

Notes:

- These turn out perfect if you make the day before. Refrigerate. Bake 30 minutes, uncovered.
- Walmart is $.57 for fresh cilantro, stand it in a jar in frig with 1" water. It will last two weeks.
- Enchiladas are traditionally made with corn tortillas, but in this dish, we prefer flour.

"A recipe has no soul, You, as the cook, must bring soul to the recipe." _Thomas Keller

Casually Created DINNERS

"One cannot think well, love well, sleep well, if one has not dined well." _Virginia Woolf

Contents:

SLOW COOKED SHORT RIBS	129
KOREAN BEEF	130
SALISBURY STEAKS	133
SLOPPY JOE BOWLS	134
FRENCH DIP WITH AU JUS	137
CHEESEBURGER SOUP	138
HOMEMADE STROGANOFF	141
GARLIC CHICKEN CAESAR WRAPS	142
CROCKPOT HAM W/ CAROLINA GOLD	145
SAUSAGE TORTELLINI BAKE	146
LASAGNA SOUP	149
STICKY CHICKEN & PINEAPPLE RICE	150
CHICKEN SCAMPI	153
CHICKEN PIE WITH PUFF PASTRY	154
CHICKEN GYROS	157
BLUE RIDGE CLUB	158
CHICKEN PARMESAN	161
FRIDAY NIGHT CHICKEN SANDWICH	163
BAKED HADDOCK WITH CRAB STUFFING	165
HONEY SRIRACHA SHRIMP	166

Slow-Cooked Beef SHORT RIBS

Short ribs are beef. You pay for a lot of bone but the flavor is really good. Depending on where you buy them, the butcher will cut them two different ways. Either way they are cut you can cook them exactly the same. If they are cut the long way (English Cut)- you will have a long bone with meat on the top side. If they are cut the short way (Flanken Cut)- you will have little circles of cut bone in your strip of meat. I like the long bones. They are beautiful when cooked.

Heat oven 325° 4 hours total	Serves: 4

MEAT:
5lb. beef short rib

RUB:
1 tsp. Paprika
1 tsp garlic powder
1 tsp onion powder
1 tsp salt
1 tsp Cumin
1 tsp black pepper

1 cup BBQ Sauce

1.) Heat oven to 325°.
2.) Line baking sheet with foil.
3.) Pat meat dry with paper towel.
4.) Combine seasoning and sprinkle on top and bottom of meat.
5.) Place in baking dish with bones on the bottom and cover tightly with foil.
6.) Cook 3-1/2 hours. The meat should be falling off the bone tender. Baste with one cup of BBQ sauce. Bake for another 20 minutes UNCOVERED.
7.) NOTE: at this point you can tightly cover these back up and let sit as long as you need before you serve them.
8.) For the perfect look- Just before serving, place under broiler just until sauce starts to caramelize and burn on the edges.

NOTES:
Here's an option that is also a favorite: Make gravy from the meat drippings and serve gourmet with mashed potatoes. Serve with mashed potatoes on the bottom, then place 1 rib of meat, then cover with gravy.

"It's always the simple that produces the marvelous." _Amelia Barr

KOREAN BEEF
with Pickled Cucumbers

I ALWAYS SAID I WOULD NEVER BE ONE OF THOSE WIVES SCRAMBLING FOR DINNER. WELL, GUESS WHAT? LIFE HAPPENS. YOUR KID HAS A TOOTH ACHE AND THE DENTIST CAN SEE HIM AT 2:00. YOU LEAVE AND FORGET TO PUT THE MEAT IN THE CROCKPOT AND WHAT'S FOR DINNER? I KNOW, AND THE DENTIST CHARGED SO MUCH YOU DON'T DARE GET TAKEOUT… GRAB THIS MEAL AND RUN WITH IT. IT'S SOLID PROTEIN AND CREATIVE VEGETABLES. GET YOUR FAVORITE RICE STARTED FIRST; THE REST WILL BE DONE IN 15 MINUTES.

Skillet	Serves 4

MEAT:
½ cup chopped onion
1 lb. ground beef

¼ cup soy sauce
¼ cup water
2 TBSP tomato paste
2 TBSP honey
2-3 cloves fresh garlic
1 tsp ground ginger
½ tsp crushed red pepper flakes
2 tsp sesame oil

PICKLED VEGGIES:
2-1/2 cups sliced cucumbers
4 tsp rice vinegar
4 tsp soy sauce
1 TBSP sugar
¼ tsp salt
1-2 cloves garlic
½ tsp black sesame seeds

1.) Put rice cooking in oven or rice cooker. If you want a recipe for rice, use page 151. Exchange pineapple juice for water if you need to.
2.) VEGGIES: Chop cucumbers and mix in a small bowl with seasonings and set aside.
3.) Heat skillet. Brown ground beef and onion. Drain.
4.) Add to skillet: soy sauce, water, tomato, honey, garlic, ginger, pepper flakes, and sesame oil.
5.) Simmer at least five minutes so the seasoning gets cooked into the meat.
6.) Garnish your bowls up pretty any way you like. We use Sriracha, cilantro, red cabbage, pickled onions…….

NOTES:
- This is a super quick meal. Tip: I always make double batches of rice and freeze it. Zap in the microwave, or thaw on counter.
- The pickled vegetables are better than you think. Try this with half carrot and half cucumbers.

"Don't quit on a bad day; only quit on a good day." _HJM

130 | PAGE

SALISBURY STEAKS
in Brown Gravy

THERE IS JUST SOMETHING SPECIAL ABOUT A MEAL THAT HAS MASHED POTATOES AND GRAVY. IT SHOWS THAT YOU REALLY WANTED SOMEONE TO COME AND YOU TOOK TIME TO PREPARE ON THEIR BEHALF. THIS IS A MEAL THAT YOU CAN HARDLY RUIN. IT WILL RETURN COMPLIMENTS TO THE COOK. IF YOU NEED TO LEAVE THIS IN THE OVEN, I HAVE BAKED IT ON 250 FOR 2-1/2 HOURS AND IT'S BEEN FINE. YOU CAN PREPARE THE DAY BEFORE, OR YOU CAN MAKE A DOUBLE BATCH AND FREEZE HALF. BOTH REHEAT WELL.

Heat 350º - 40 minutes - Covered	9x13 pan - Serves 6-8

Meat:
- 2 lb. hamburger
- 2 eggs
- 1 tsp pepper
- 1 tsp salt
- 1 tsp garlic powder
- 1 cup breadcrumbs
- ½ cup chopped onion

- 2 TBSP oil for browning

Gravy
- 3 packages brown gravy mix

Garnish with fresh Thyme (optional)

1.) Put thawed hamburger in mixing bowl and add eggs, pepper, salt, garlic, breadcrumbs, and chopped onion. Mix until combined. Do not overmix.
2.) Divide meat in 8 patties (about 2/3 cup each). Shape into hamburger style patties.
3.) In non-stick skillet, heat 1 TBSP oil and brown four patties at a time. Flip and brown the other side. Repeat with the other four patties.
4.) Place in a sprayed 9x13 pan.
5.) Prepare gravy according to package directions and pour over steaks.
6.) Cover tightly. Bake.
7.) Serve with mashed potatoes.

NOTES:
- I always make my own breadcrumbs. Use frozen bread from the freezer (Best way to get rid of hamburger buns). Grate frozen bread on a cheese grater. You got it.
- You can make the gravy from scratch with flour, butter, beef bouillon, and gravy browning, but it adds a lot of steps, and I like to make this quick. The meat and mashed potatoes already take a lot of time.

"The bad news is, time flies. The good news is you're the pilot." _Michael Altshuler

SLOPPY JOE BOWLS *with Sweet Potatoes*

We are a very traditional meat-eating family, but I'm always on a mission to eat less white flour. Sloppy Joe's are a personal favorite, and this is a guilt free way to eat them. Some of my boys do not like sweet potatoes so I do one pan of white potatoes and one pan of sweet. Use the same amount of oil and seasoning for either kind potato. The toppings for this bowl are endless. On the next page is a quick slaw recipe that is great on this dish.

Heat oven 425° - 35 minutes	Serves 6

Meat:
- 1-1/2 lb. ground turkey
- ¾ cup diced onion
- 6 oz. can tomato paste
- 1 cup water
- 2 TBSP taco seasoning
- 1 tsp garlic powder
- 1 tsp black pepper
- 1 tsp salt
- 4 tsp brown sugar
- 1 TBSP Worcestershire sauce

Potatoes:
- 3 large, sweet potatoes
- 2 TBSP oil
- ½ tsp salt after roasting

Toppings:
- Sliced Jalapenos
- Shredded cheese
- Sour cream
- Chives
- Pickled onions
- Cilantro

1.) Start the potatoes first. Wash. Cut in 1" cubes (I don't peel). Place on parchment lined baking sheet.
2.) Drizzle oil over potatoes and toss with your hands to coat. Bake uncovered 35 minutes. Salt potatoes after cooking to help ensure crispiness.
3.) In large skillet, brown onion and turkey. I don't drain. Add all seasonings. Simmer 5-10 minutes.
4.) Chop up toppings
5.) If making slaw, mix together right before serving.

NOTES:
- Always cook enough meat for two meals. It will save you time.
- FYI ground turkey is 22 g. protein per serving.

"Some people say, 'You are what you eat; others say, 'You are what you digest'." _Karen Coponen

FAVORITE SLAW:

1-1/2 lb. chopped cabbage (1/2 head)
½ cup mayonnaise
2 TBSP jalapeno juice
¾ tsp garlic salt
½ tsp black pepper
1 tsp sugar

Put all ingredients in a medium bowl. Stir to combine, just before serving.

"This French Dip is super easy to make.
After you take your first bite, you can't put it down."
Ashlyn and Eli Coponen – Campobello, SC

FRENCH DIP *with Au Jus*

The French Dip sandwich, is not French at all. It was first served in public at a Los Angeles restaurant in California in 1908. In 2007 Cole's Restaurant was completely refurbished and I have heard it is a great historical building. It's on my bucket list to go there.

"Au Jus" • oh zhoos is a French word, and it simply means, "With juice."

Crockpot – High 5-6 hours	Serves 6-8

Meat:
4-5 lb. chuck roast
Salt and pepper
1 TBSP olive oil

2 cans beef consommé
2 cans hot water
1 onion, cut in rings
5 TBSP soy sauce
1 teaspoon garlic powder
½ tsp black pepper

Meat:
8 French rolls
Butter rolls
8 slices provolone cheese

1.) In skillet, heat oil. Salt and pepper roast. Brown 5 minutes on each side.
2.) In crockpot, combine consommé, water, onion, soy sauce, garlic, and pepper.
3.) Place browned roast in crockpot.
4.) Cover tightly, cook on high 5-6 hours; Cook until fork tender. Let rest in juice until ready to serve. (this can even be a couple of hours).
5.) When ready to eat. Set meat on a cutting board and rest it for 10 minutes (this helps the meat absorb its own juice). While waiting for meat, cut rolls, butter, toast under broiler, add cheese, melt under broiler.
6.) Cut meat with a sharp knife or pull it apart with two forks. Lay on toasted rolls.
7.) Serve on a plate, with a small bowl of au jus from crock pot.

NOTES:
- I like to brown my meat after lunch and put in the crockpot on high. (Takes less than 10 minutes to put together). You have a beautiful supper ready in 15 minutes when you get home.

CHEESEBURGER *Soup*

Comfort, Comfort, Comfort Food! This is the soup you want in your crockpot when you come home from church on a cold rainy Sunday. Pair with my favorite cheese dunkers and you are open for business. By the way, this is serious guy food! However, if you need this on the healthier side, you can secretly add diced celery and yellow squash and it disguises well!

| Stovetop | Serves 5 (2 cup) servings. |

Large Pot:
2 TBSP Olive Oil
1 small onion (3/4) cup diced
1 pound ground beef

1 large carrot (1 cup) diced
4 potatoes (4 cups) diced
3 cups chicken broth (with salt)
1 tsp basil
½ tsp salt
½ tsp black pepper
½ tsp garlic powder

Non-stick Pan:
4 TBSP butter
¼ cup flour
1-1/2 cups milk
½ cup sour cream
1 cup cheddar cheese
10 slices American cheese

1.) Heat olive oil in large soup pot. Sauté onions for one minute. Add hamburger, brown, and drain.
2.) Add diced potatoes (with peelings), carrots, broth, and seasonings.
3.) Cover and simmer 15 minutes.
4.) While meat and veggies are simmering, combine white sauce in non-stick pan.
5.) Melt butter, whisk in flour, whisk in milk and bring to a boil for one minute.
6.) If you are serving right away, add sour cream and cheeses to white sauce. Whisk till smooth. Add to soup pot and keep warm. Do NOT boil.
7.) If you are making this soup ahead do not add sour cream or cheeses until it has been reheated.

NOTES:
Soups with cream or sour cream should never be boiled or they will curd. Always add just before serving or when hot enough to eat.

"Let's spoon together and share some soup love." _Unknown

DIPPING CROUTONS:

4 Hamburger buns
Butter lightly both sides.
Sprinkle with garlic salt.

Cut into 1"x1-1/2" pieces. Toss on baking sheet. Toast under broiler till golden brown. Do not multitask.

"Quick and cozy weeknight soup! Everyone enjoyed this!" Naomi Kaiser – Campobello, SC

"Comfort food at its finest! I was begged to make it every day, it's that good!."
Alyssa Matson – Yacolt, WA

Homemade Stroganoff
with French Fried Onions

There is nothing like comfort food, and when you are sick, the simpler the food the better. When I was sick with covid, our North Carolina church family was phenomenal. They dropped food on our front porch. I just remember the simplicity of some of those meals, and it really made me think, how, "less is more". It was all I could eat. I love to bring this meal to people! It's easy to double up and make a pan for your house while you're at it.

Bake 400° 15 minutes - Uncovered	9x13 Serves 6-8

Ingredients:

- 1 lb. hamburger
- ½ cup chopped onion
- 8oz. egg noodles
- 4 TBSP butter
- 1 cup chopped mushrooms (optional)
- 1 TBSP minced garlic
- 2 tsp Worcestershire sauce
- ¾ tsp black pepper
- 1 TBSP dried parsley
- 4 tsp beef bouillon
- 2 TBSP flour
- 3 cups water
- 1 cup sour cream
- 1 cup French's onions

1.) Cook noodles according to package directions.
2.) Chop onion and brown with hamburger. Drain. Set aside.
3.) In skillet, melt butter. If using mushrooms add now. Sauté mushrooms 5 minutes. Add garlic. Add Worcestershire, pepper, parsley, bouillon, and flour. Stir until combined.
4.) Add water and bring to a boil. Boil three minutes. Add in drained noodles, hamburger, and sour cream. Stir to combine.
5.) Spread in a 9x13 pan and top with French's onions.
6.) Bake uncovered 15 minutes.
7.) Serve.

NOTES:
- Garnish with grated parmesan cheese.
- Make the day before and add an extra ½ cup of water.

"Nobody can go back and start a new beginning, but anyone can start today and make a new ending." _Maria Robinson

Caesar Wraps with GARLIC CHICKEN

Caesar salad originated in 1924 by an Italian immigrant Caesar Cardini. He lived in San Diego, CA, but ran a restaurant in Tijuana, Mexico. It is said, the dish was invented when the kitchen ran out of ingredients for another dish. I just think it's funny, that an Italian, from America, invented this dish, in his Mexican restaurant.

Heat large skillet.	4 large servings

Meat:
2 large uncooked chicken breasts
4 TBSP butter
1 tsp garlic powder
1 tsp salt
4 Tbsp fine Parmesan cheese
4 Tbsp chopped fresh parsley

Ingredients:
4 large flour tortillas (10")
1 ripe avocado
1 recipe of Caesar salad page 70
(I do put the croutons)
Red onion
Roma tomatoes

1) Divide all the ingredients for chicken into two piles. You will cook this in 2 batches. Slice raw chicken breast ¼" thick. Heat large skillet till (2 TBSP) butter is sizzling.
2) Place single layer of chicken in pan; sprinkle with ¼ tsp garlic, ¼ tsp salt, 1 TBSP of cheese, and 1 TBSP fresh parsley. Turn in 3 minutes.
3) Sprinkle the second side with the same. Cook 3 more minutes. Double check for doneness or 160°.
4) Repeat steps 2 and 3 for remaining chicken. Chop chicken.
5) Arrange wrap: Tortilla, avocado, Caesar salad, chicken, red onion, and tomato.
6) Fold in each end about 2". Press down firmly and roll.
7) Place on foil or wax paper. Wrap. Then cut sandwich in half.

NOTES:
- My favorite side with this is the Best Oven Fries on page 91. When they are almost done cooking, add the salt and ½ tsp dried Rosemary.

"A coward dies a thousand deaths; the gallant never taste death but once." _Julius Caesar

CAROLINA GOLD SAUCE

½ cup yellow mustard
¾ cup brown sugar
¾ cup honey
¼ cup apple cider vinegar
1 tsp Sriracha
2 TBSP ketchup
2 tsp Worcestershire Sauce
1 tsp garlic powder
1/8 tsp cayenne

Put all ingredients in a small pot and bring to a boil. Simmer 3 minutes. Cool. Store in an airtight container.

CROCKPOT HAM
with Carolina Gold

COOKING HAM IS A LIFE SKILL. IT IS ECONOMICAL AND YOU CAN HARDLY RUIN IT. IT IS SUPER EASY. DO YOU KNOW ALL THE THINGS YOU CAN DO WITH HAM? YOU CAN SERVE IT TRADITIONAL WITH MASHED POTATOES AND GRAVY, OR BBQ STYLE WITH BAKED BEANS AND BISCUIT. YOU CAN ALSO CHOP IT LIKE PULLED PORK FOR BBQ SANDWICHES (THIS IS A GREAT WAY TO FEED A CROWD). IT'S GREAT IN MORE BREAKFAST DISHES THAN I CAN COUNT, SCALLOPED POTATOES, SOUPS, AND THAT NAMES A FEW.

Crockpot 6-quart size/6-7 hours (high)	Serves 6-8

INGREDIENTS:

7 lb. bone-in ham (Always buy the 'butt' portion instead of the 'shank'. The shank is cheaper, but the bone and waste is so much more, it is NOT cheaper.

CAROLINE GOLD SAUCE:

See left.

For Favorite Slaw see page 135

1.) Place ham in crockpot cut side down. This puts the fat on top.
2.) Add 1 cup of water.
3.) Place in crockpot on high 6-7 hours, or until you can pull it apart with a fork.
4.) When meat is done, remove from broth and let stand on a cutting board. If you don't want to burn your hands, you may want to wait 30 minutes to shred the meat.
5.) This recipe suggests pulled ham sandwiches, but the Carolina gold is perfect for a BBQ style meal as well.
6.) Mix the gold sauce and pour in a sauce bottle. Drizzle generously.

NOTES:

- Put leftover meat in freezer bags. Label. Always have precooked meat on hand. You can have a meal ready in 15 minutes.

"The happiest people don't have the best of everything, they make the best of everything." _Unknown

TORTELLINI BAKE
with Sausage

We have a large family, so when we travel, I prepare the meals before we go and then just reheat them when we are there. I like that, because it feels like I get a vacation, and you don't have to break the bank for food. Even if you don't care about costs, wait times are annoying and I hate seeing my kids eat French fries twice a day. I came up with this casserole when I was fixing food for Amanda's graduation trip to Pensacola.

Heat oven 350⁰ - 25 minutes	Serves 6-8

Ingredients:

- 1 lb. sausage
- ½ cup onion chopped
- 4 tsp minced garlic

- 1 28oz. can crushed tomatoes
- 1 (6oz.) can tomato paste
- 2 cups water
- 4 tsp Italian seasoning
- 1 tsp garlic salt
- 1 tsp black pepper
- 2 tsp chicken bouillon
- 3 TBSP dill pickle juice

- 3 lbs. tortellini (your choice of filling)
- 1 cup grated parmesan
- ¼ cup chopped fresh basil

1.) In deep skillet- sauté sausage, onions, and garlic.
2.) Add in crushed tomatoes, paste, water, seasonings, and pickle juice.
3.) Bring to a steaming simmer. Add in tortellini. Finish cooking it whichever way works best for you:
   a. Simmer 15 minutes. Serve.
   b. Bake in the oven on 350⁰ covered 25 minutes.
   c. Place in crockpot on low 3-4 hours.
   d. Freeze and reheat when needed.
4.) Garnish with basil and parmesan right before serving.

NOTES:

- These cooking times are with refrigerated tortellini. May need to add 10 minutes to the simmer if using frozen.
- I buy cheese tortellini, but you can use whatever filling you prefer.
- Serve it up with garlic bread, Caesar salad, and cold soda.

"Fill your life with experiences, not things. Have stories to tell, not stuff to show". bumper-sticker

Three Cheese LASAGNA SOUP

This is a hearty soup that leaves you feeling like you ate a real meal. You can put this together in less than 15 minutes. Since the cheese is not added until you serve it, it is very crockpot friendly. This is also a recipe you can make if you need a vegetarian meal. Omit sausage and sauté zucchini, mushrooms, and yellow squash with onions and garlic.

Heat – Stovetop 6 qt kettle	Serves 6-8

Ingredients:

- 1 lb. ground sausage
- 1 cup chopped onion
- 3 cloves fresh garlic
- 1 (28oz.) can crushed tomatoes
- 1 (6 oz.) can tomato paste
- 7 cups chicken broth
- 1 tsp salt
- 1 tsp pepper
- 1 tsp sugar
- 4 tsp Italian seasoning
- 9 (half box) lasagna noodles
- 2 cups spinach

- 10 oz. ricotta cheese
- 1 cup mozzarella cheese
- ½ parmesan cheese
- 2 tsp dried parsley

1.) In a six-quart soup pot, brown sausage and onion. Drain. Add in garlic and cook for 1 more minute.
2.) Add tomatoes, broth, salt, pepper, sugar, Italian seasoning, and noodles (break noodles into 1" pieces). Simmer 30 minutes.
3.) If making ahead of time, I don't add the spinach till right before I serve.
4.) In a separate bowl mix together cheeses and parsley. Refrigerate till ready to serve.
5.) CROCKPOT: If you want to put this in the crockpot, cook sausage, onions, and garlic. Transfer to crockpot and follow directions as above. 3-4 hours on high.
6.) Serve soup very hot with a cookie scoop of cheese mixture in the middle of bowl.

NOTE:

- If making the day before, do not add noodles until you are ready to serve. Bring your base to a boil, add noodles, boil 15 minutes, add spinach, and serve.

"Today I will be as useless as the 'G' in lasagna" _@Mypostcard

STICKY CHICKEN
with Pineapple Rice

Pineapple-rice sounds scary gourmet, but it's not. It is a subtil light flavor that most people wouldn't recognize. It complements the chicken, and if you grill the pineapple rings, it makes a well-rounded dish. My boys love this dish, and I always serve it with the Japanese Steakhouse sauce on page 96. I don't recommend making ahead.

Heat	Serves 6

Sauce:
½ cup butter
1 cup brown sugar
1 TBSP minced garlic
1/3 cup soy sauce
1/3 cup orange juice

Meat:
2 lb. chicken breast
¾ cup flour
4 TBSP butter

Pineapple Slices:
2 TBSP butter
Pineapple rings from one can
3 TBSP brown sugar
Pinch of salt

Red Peppers:
1 red bell pepper, sliced
Dash of oil

1.) SAUCE: Combine all sauce ingredients and boil 3-4 minutes until sauce caramelizes. Set aside.
2.) PINEAPPLE: Melt butter. Add brown sugar. Heat till bubbly. Place pineapple in caramel mixture till brown on one side. Flip and brown the second side.
3.) PEPPERS: Heat Skillet. Sauté peppers 3-4 minutes. Salt to taste. Set aside.
4.) CHICKEN: Slice chicken in 1/8 "slices. Place in a Zip Lock bag and shake with flour.
5.) Heat half of butter in a large skillet, on really high heat and add half of chicken. Spread in a single layer. Cook about 3 minutes. Flip and cook 2 more minutes. Add ¼ cup of sauce and let it start to caramelize and burn onto the meat. I start chopping the meat with an egg turner. This cuts it into small pieces.
6.) Repeat step five

Notes:
I put the rice cooking, then make sauce, pineapple, peppers, then the meat. It should all be ready by the time the rice is done cooking.

PINEAPPLE RICE

2 cups long grain white rice
Juice from 1 (15oz.) can pineapple (this is usually about 7/8 of a cup)
3 cups water
1 tsp salt
2 TBSP butter

Spray 9x13 pan. Mix all ingredients. Use hot water (saves 10 minutes cooking time) (butter can be lumpy). Cover tightly. Bake on 350° for 30 minutes.

"Burning the sauce onto the chicken adds a depth we always miss when we make teriyaki chicken at home. I will be trying every recipe is this chapter."
Katie Lampinen – Washington State

CHICKEN SCAMPI
with Angel Hair Pasta

I HAVE ALWAYS WONDERED WHAT IS SCAMPI ABOUT SCAMPI? SO, THE SHORT STORY IS: ITALIAN IMMIGRANTS COULD NOT FIND THEIR TRADITIONAL SHELLFISH "LANGOUSTINES" IN THE US. "SCAMPI" IS THE PLURAL WORD FOR SCAMPO, THE ITALIAN NAME FOR LANGOUSTINES. WITH THAT BEING SAID, CHICKEN SCAMPI IS JUST AN EVOLUTION FROM SHRIMP SCAMPI FOR THOSE NOT WANTING SHELLFISH.

Heat in skillet	Serves 6

CHICKEN:
- 1-1/2 lb. chicken tenders (raw)
- 2 TBSP butter
- ½ cup flour
- ½ tsp salt

VEGGIES:
- 2 bell peppers
- 1 medium onion
- 1 TBSP butter

SAUCE:
- 2 TBSP butter
- 3 med garlic cloves
- 3 TBSP flour
- 3 cups chicken broth
- 1 tsp salt
- 1 tsp coarse pepper
- 1 TBSP fresh lemon juice
- 1 tsp dried basil
- ½ tsp oregano
- 2 tsp dried parsley
- 1/3 cup cream

PASTA:
- 12 oz. angel hair pasta
- ¾ cup parmesan cheese

1.) CHICKEN: Melt butter in hot skillet. Mix flour and salt together and dip chicken. Fry in butter about 3 minutes each side or 160°. Set aside.

2.) VEGGIES: Thinly slice bell peppers and onions. Sauté in butter. Set aside.

3.) SAUCE: Melt butter, sauté garlic 1 minute, add flour, stir into a crumble, slowly add chicken broth. Whisk until smooth. Add seasonings: salt, pepper, lemon, basil, oregano, parsley, and cream.

4.) PASTA: Cook pasta according to package directions. Drain.

5.) Layer on serving platter with pasta, sauce, chicken, veggies, and parmesan cheese.

6.) This is a beautiful dish. It can be served alone, or with salad and breadsticks.

"Through all the waiting, hoping, planning, worrying, praying, trusting, crying, and celebrating, we become the mothers God wants us to be" _Heidi St. John

Flaky CHICKEN PIE

Mid-Century chicken pie was made with a top and bottom pastry crust. It was filled with meat and gravy. It usually had a lot of spices and herbs. This was significant in that it was a way to preserve meat without refrigeration. Today we refrigerate so, it's common to have variations from the traditional. The other way I make this dish is to use biscuits instead of phyllo. The secret if you want to try biscuits is: bake your biscuits at least halfway before putting them on top.

| Heat 325° - 25 minutes | Serves 9x13 pan or 10" skillet |

Filling:

- 1 quart chicken broth
- 4 chicken breasts (boneless skinless) appx. 2-1/2 lb.
- 2 cups chopped carrots
- 1 cup diced celery
- 1 cup diced onion

- 1 stick butter (1/2 cup)
- ½ tsp salt
- 1 tsp pepper
- 1 tsp garlic
- ½ tsp thyme
- 1 TBSP dried parsley
- 1/3 cup flour

- 1 package phyllo dough
- 4 TBSP butter
- ¼ tsp coarse salt

1.) Take phyllo dough out of freezer and unbox to thaw. Set aside.
2.) Cut raw chicken in bite size pieces.
3.) Place chicken broth in saucepan. Bring to a boil. When boiling, add chicken, carrots, celery, and onion. Bring back to a boil and then simmer 15 minutes.
4.) In a large skillet melt butter, add pepper, garlic, thyme, parsley, and flour. Stir to form a buttery paste. Add to chicken, broth, and vegetables. Stir to form a thick gravy.
5.) Pour in a 9x13 pan.
6.) Melt 4 TBSP butter and lightly brush each sheet of phyllo dough (you can only do one at a time). Scrunch in a ball to form a flower. Repeat for each sheet of phyllo. Sprinkle with salt.

NOTES:

- For a quicker option, use the meat from one rotisserie chicken (that's about 2 lbs.) Cook in the same manner as above and omit salt.
- Phyllo dough is found with frozen Cool Whip and desserts in the freezer section of the grocery store.

"It is better to fail in originality than to succeed in imitation." _Herman Melville

Tzatziki (tsäˈtsēkē) Sauce

¾ cup yogurt
¾ cup sour cream
1 TBSP minced garlic
1 cucumber (1 cup)
2 TBSP olive oil
1 TBSP lemon juice
1 tsp black pepper
1 TBSP dried dill
1 tsp salt

Peel cucumber, scrape out seeds, and dice into ¼ inch pieces or smaller. Combine all ingredients. Stir to combine. Store in refrigerator up to one week. This is best with fresh dill, but fresh is hard to find.

Freaky Geeky CHICKEN GYRO (YEE-roh)

It's like, "Who even wants to cook something you can't pronounce!" I get that, but this is a super fun creative meal with so many flavors and so many options. You will be making three different recipes: Naan Bread, Tzatziki Sauce, Chicken. I suggest you: Make Naan bread dough. While it's rising, cook the chicken and set aside, make the sauce and refrigerate, chop your garnishes and cook the naan last.

Heat Skillet	Serves

Naan Breads:
- ½ cup warm water
- 2 tsp instant yeast
- 1 tsp sugar
- 3 TBSP olive oil
- ¼ cup plain yogurt
- 1 egg
- ½ tsp salt
- 2-1/2 – 3 cups flour

Toppings:
- Avacado slices
- Pickled red onions
- Shredded lettuce
- Diced tomatoes

1.) Combine warm water, yeast, and sugar in a large bowl. Let sit 5 minutes. Add olive oil, yogurt, egg, salt, and 2 cups of flour. Stir till smooth.
2.) Knead with mixer or by hand. Add enough flour to make a soft dough.
3.) Cover dough and let rise 20-30 minutes.
4.) Preheat skillet to medium heat.
5.) Cut dough in 8 pieces. Dust a cutting board with flour. Roll out into 6" circles.
6.) Drizzle a little oil in the pan. Cook naan 2-3 minutes, flip when bubbly and golden brown. Cook the other side 2-3 minutes. Reduce heat if they brown too quickly.

NOTES:
- These must be eaten as soon as they are assembled.
- <u>For chicken recipe see page 101</u>. Place chicken on ½ of naan, toppings on top the chicken, drizzle with Tzatziki, and fold naan in half. Should resemble a taco.
- Naans can be made ahead and frozen.

"The power of finding beauty in the humblest things makes home happy and life lovely." _Louisa May Alcott

BLUE RIDGE CLUB
with Basil Aioli

"It's in the sauce," That's the best description you can get for this sandwich. At the same time, I'll give a few hints to make this sandwich epic: Costco has the best croissants. Buy good smoked turkey breast. Use good mayo in the sauce. Use Havarti cheese. Bread must be toasted. Find good friends to share it with, and if you live anywhere near North Carolina, picnic in our Blue Ridge Mountains; and if you don't, Take time to picnic wherever you live.

Broiler/Camp stove	Serves 6

SANDWICH:
6 large croissants
9 slices Havarti cheese
1-1/2 lb. smoked turkey breast

BASIL AIOLI:
1 cup mayonnaise
2 tsp lemon juice
¼ tsp salt
½ cup fresh chopped basil (loosely packed)
1 medium clove fresh garlic
¼ tsp coarse black pepper
¼ tsp dried Rosemary

TOPPINGS:
Arugula or fresh greens
Thin sliced Kosher dill pickles

1.) AIOLI: Place all ingredients in blender or food processor. Pulse till smooth. Scrape into a bowl.
2.) Cut open croissants. Lightly butter. Toast under broiler at home, or we improvise on the camp stove.
3.) Over toasted croissant, place 4 oz. smoked turkey on one half and 1-1/2 slices of cheese on the other. Return to oven to melt cheese and warm meat.
4.) Spread 2 TBSP aioli on meat. Place a slice of pickle and then the arugula.
5.) Cut in half and serve immediately.

NOTES:
- We love fresh garlic and basil, but if that's not in the plan, then make this anyway, and use ½ tsp garlic powder and 1 tsp dried basil.
- These are also really good on Brioche buns.
- "Aioli" is just a fancy name for seasoned mayonnaise. So yummy!
- You either love or hate arugula, so use whatever greens you like.

"That awkward moment at a Feminist picnic when they realized no one had made any sandwiches" _Let's hope that's not us.

Homemade Marinara Sauce:

2 TBSP olive oil
½ cup onion finely chopped
4 tsp minced garlic
3 (14.5oz.) cans diced tomatoes
2 tsp basil
2 tsp oregano
1 tsp sugar
2 tsp salt
1 tsp black pepper
2 tsp chicken bouillon
2 TBSP dill pickle juice

Sauté onion in oil for 5 minutes. Add garlic.
Blend tomatoes in blender or food processor; add to onions.
Add all seasonings. Simmer all ingredients 5-10 minutes.

CHICKEN PARMESAN
with Pasta & Marinara

Quick and Easy — Dinner Must be Done

I didn't make chicken parmesan for 15 years because it was too much work, fillet the chicken, pound it out to tenderize. Might be dry, might be tough..... Heidi got the genius idea to use the tenders. They cost a bit more but it's so worth it. You can make this from scratch and add it to the list of quick meals. Another note: Panko just came out with gluten free (rice) breadcrumbs. Add the extra seasoning below and you have gluten free chicken parmesan!

Oven to 425º - Make 18 min. + 5 min.	Serves 6

Chicken:
- 1/3 cup flour
- 1/3 cup parmesan cheese
- 1/3 cup seasoned breadcrumbs
- ½ tsp salt
- 1 tsp pepper
- 1 tsp garlic powder

- 5 TBSP butter (melted)
- 1-1/2 lb. chicken tenders (raw)

Pasta:
- 12 oz. spaghetti
- 2 TBSP Olive oil
- ½ tsp garlic salt

Marinara:
- Large jar of favorite marinara (You need 2 cups for top of chicken. I like extra).
- 1 cup mozzarella cheese

1.) Combine flour, parmesan cheese, breadcrumbs, salt, pepper, and garlic powder.
2.) Don't rinse chicken. Coat with melted butter and then coat with bread crumb mixture. Place on a parchment paper lined baking sheet. Bake 18 minutes uncovered (160º internal temp.).
3.) Remove from oven and cover each tender with 1-1/2 TBSP marinara. Sprinkle cheese evenly over the top of chicken. Return to the oven and bake just until cheese is evenly melted. (appx. 5 minutes).
4.) While chicken is baking, boil pasta according to package directions. Drain. Add olive oil and garlic salt.
5.) Garnish with extra sauce and fresh parsley.

NOTES:
- If you want to use homemade sauce, see page 160.
- If you don't have seasoned breadcrumbs, add ¼ tsp dried basil and ¼ tsp dried oregano to plain.

"Nothing is impossible, the word itself says 'I'm possible'." _Audrey Hepburn

HOMEMADE SRIRACHA SAUCE

1/3 cup sriracha
½ cup honey
2 TBSP butter

Bring sriracha and honey to a boil. Boil 2 minutes. Remove from heat and stir in butter till smooth. Cool. Serve. Refrigerate.

TGI Friday CHICKEN SANDWICH

In our last book we had the **TGI Friday Chicken Fingers**. We loved and you loved it. When we were testing recipes for this book, one of my daughters said, "The sandwich is going to be my TGI Friday in the New Book." I laughed when she said that. The next day, I renamed the sandwich. Why not? It's the same idea! Keep it simple. Keep it home. Keep it fun. Keep it yummy.

Stovetop	Serves 6-8

Sandwich:
6 Bare brand chicken breasts
4 slices favorite cheese (we use Havarti)
6 Brioche buns buttered (Aldi has the best price)

Sauce:
1 cup mayonnaise
2 TBSP BBQ sauce
2 TBSP honey
2 tsp mustard
1 tsp granulated onion
½ tsp coarse pepper
½ tsp garlic powder

Toppings:
Washed romaine lettuce
Sliced tomato

1.) Place chicken on parchment covered baking sheet. Bake according to package directions.
2.) Mix up sauce and set aside.
3.) Wash lettuce. Set aside.
4.) Slice tomato.
5.) Prepare other sides and get dinner dishes etc. ready. You want to eat when the chicken is done.
6.) Get drinks ready.
7.) Grill Buns.
8.) Place cheese on chicken pieces right before they are done.
9.) Build sandwiches.
10.) Happy Friday!

NOTES:
- The "Bare" brand chicken is found at Sam's Club, Costco, our local Food Lion has it. It is worth the extra money and is an item that goes on sale.
- My favorite sides are homemade fries page 91, and my Mom's Jello Salad page 81.
- Surprise your family with the super quick Chocolate Chip Cookie Bars on page 198.

"The Fridayest Friday that ever Fridayed was the Friday after a Thursday you thought was Friday." _AAT

BAKED HADDOCK
with Crab Stuffing

Did you ever order a stuffed seafood dish and it came with the stuffing on top? Well, that's very normal. Fish tends to break apart when cooked. If you use a thin fish like Tilapia, you can roll the whole fillet. That is pretty, but the servings are large and you need a meat thermometer to make sure they are done in the middle. I prefer the stuffing on top so it gets crispy. Haddock is an east coast fish. You would use Pacific Cod on the west coast.

Heat oven 400° - 20 minutes	Serves 6

Fish:
- 2 lbs. of fish fillets
- 2 cups milk
- Olive oil for rubbing
- Salt and pepper
- 3 TBSP butter

Stuffing:
- ¼ cup butter
- 3 cloves garlic
- ¼ cup green onion, chopped
- ½ tsp coarse pepper
- ¼ tsp salt
- ½ tsp ground sage
- 1 can minced crab with juice
- 1 cup plain breadcrumbs

1. Cut fish in 2-3" fillets. Place in gallon zip lock bag with milk. Let sit 20 minutes. While resting, make stuffing.
2. STUFFING: in skillet- melt butter. Sauté garlic and onion 1 minute. And pepper, salt, sage, crab, and breadcrumbs. Stir to combine. Set aside.
3. Line baking sheet with foil. Melt 3 TBSP butter on foil.
4. Remove from milk. Rinse. Dry with paper towels. Rub with olive oil. Salt and pepper. Place on baking sheet in melted butter.
5. Spoon stuffing on top of fish about ¼" thick.
6. Bake, uncovered.

NOTES:
- This is not the same if you don't use fresh garlic.
- If using seasoned breadcrumbs, omit sage.
- Soaking in milk absorbs the fish odor.
- Drying fish helps it have a flaky texture and helps it brown.
- Oiling fish keeps the inside moisture from escaping.
- Salting fish helps dry the outside; this creates less steam and improves outside and inside textures.

"No one is born a great cook; one learns by doing." Julia Child

HONEY SRIRACHA SHRIMP
with Green Peas

We were recently staying at someone's house and they wanted me to make salmon. They do not cook much and there was not many ingredients on hand. I pretty much made this sauce and marinated the salmon in it. It turned out excellent, but I kept telling Dave, "This sauce wants to be on shrimp." So, I came home an tried it and it's a new favorite.

Heat	Serves

Shrimp:
2 lbs. raw shrimp (peeled and deveined) I buy small
Skewers 10"
Olive oil

Sauce:
1 TBSP lime juice
2 TBSP soy sauce
1 TBSP rice vinegar
4 TBSP honey
2 TBSP Sriracha
1 TBSP minced garlic

Garnish Ideas:
Sesame seeds
Green onions
Crushed red pepper flakes

Peas:
1 bag pea pods
1 TBSP oil

1.) Thaw shrimp in refrigerator or under running cold water. Drain. Pat with paper towel to dry.
2.) Place dry shrimp on skewers.
3.) Heat large skillet with 2 TBSP olive oil. When hot, place skewered shrimp in single layer. Cook 3 minutes, flip and cook three more minutes. Repeat this step till all skewers are cooked.
4.) In same skillet, combine all sauce ingredients. Bring to a boil and cook for 3-4 minutes. Submerge shrimp in sauce and serve immediately.
5.) PEAS: Heat medium skillet with 1 TBSP oil and sauté peas for three minutes on high heat. Salt to taste.
6.) <u>Serve over a bed of rice.</u> Arrange shrimp skewers, peas, and garnishes.

NOTES:
- Use rice recipe from page 150.
- Use Japanese Steakhouse sauce recipe from page 96

"There is eternal influence and power in motherhood." —Julie B. Beck

Recipe for "Grandma-hood"

"Old and grey and in the way." Is the most terrible quote ever written. I'm writing the following recipe to teach the young the value and necessity of our elders. And... if there was ever a grandma that believed this lie, this is your reminder that your work is not done. The young need your love when the rest of the world gives up on them.

Bake: 70 years	Yield: Virtue

Environment:
Morning after rain
Sidewalk
Grass along the sidewalk

Ingredients:
1 grandma
(with bad knees is ok)
1 worm

1. Take a walk, down your sidewalk, the morning after a stiff rain.
2. When you are almost home and your legs are getting a little tired, let your eyes watch the sidewalk in front of you so you don't trip.
3. When you see the little worm, washed out of the grass by the rain, you will know that if someone doesn't throw him back in the grass, he doesn't have a chance.
4. You stoop down and pick him up.
5. You toss him in the grass and wish him well.
6. If your steps weren't slow, you would have never seen him.

Notes:

Do you know anyone that says, "My grandma always loved me!"? Sometimes all we need is for one person to give us another chance.

How many times do grandma's worry about things moms don't have time to worry about?

Yes, this is a true story.

"Aging is an extraordinary process where you become the person you always should have been." _David Bowie

My sweet daughters and grand-daughters

Something Sweet

"Baking may be regarded as a science, but it's the chemistry between the ingredients and the cook that gives desserts life. Baking is done out of love, to share with family and friends, to see them smile." _Anna Olson

Contents:

Celebrate Everything Cupcakes	173
Ice Cream Sandwiches	174
Creamy Lemon Bars	177
Lemon Meringue Bliss	178
Chocolate Picnic Cookies	181
Banana Crème Torte (Cover)	182
Cappuccino Fluff	185
Raspberry Crumble Bars	186
Birthday Cake Squares	189
Hot Fudge Topping	191
Old-fashioned Shortcake	192
Chocolate Cheesecake Bars	195
Grilled Blueberry Crisp	197
Chocolate Chip Cookie Bars	198
Chocolate Skillet Cake	201
Carrot Cake	202

"They are so moist and so good! They were easy to make."
Shannon Kaiser – Castlewood, SD – Age 11

"Celebrate Everything" Cupcakes

There are very few things in life that can make someone smile like a cupcake. We use these for birthdays, gender reveals, holidays, baby meals, and you name it! Last I made these for the doctor's office that took such good care of my mom during her illness.

Bake 350° 17 Minutes	Makes 12

Cup Cakes:

- 1-1/2 cups flour
- 1 cup sugar
- ¼ cup cornstarch
- ½ tsp salt
- 2 tsp baking powder

- ½ cup butter (melted)
- 2/3 cup milk
- ½ cup sour cream
- 1 tsp vanilla extract
- 1 tsp almond extra

- ¼ cup cold water
- 3 egg whites

Frosting

- ¾ cup butter, softened
- 4 cups powdered sugar
- 1/3 cup heavy cream
- 2 tsp vanilla

1.) Grab your favorite mixing bowl and a wire whisk.
2.) In bowl, add dry ingredients. Give a quick whisk. Pour in melted butter and whisk to sticky crumbles.
3.) Add milk, sour cream, and extracts. Stir until combined.
4.) Stir in egg whites and water. Whisk till smooth.
5.) Divide into cupcake papers.
6.) Bake
7.) Cool 30 minutes before frosting.
8.) FROSTING: Whip softened butter and powdered sugar until crumbly. Add vanilla and cream. Beat at least two minutes to get light and fluffy.

NOTES:

- If you don't have a decorating tip, use a plastic Zip-Lock bag and cut the corner off about ½". This will make a nice frosting ball.
- If you need to transport these, it helps to freeze them so they don't melt in the car.

"Cupcakes are muffins that believed in miracles!" _Unknown

Ice-Cream Sandwiches

While on a Sunday drive we stopped at a darling food truck selling homemade ice cream sandwiches. We were hooked!! The next Sunday we contemplated retracing the same route. Since that wasn't really possible, and it was $35 for most of us to get a half, I started making different cookies and Dave went on an ice cream hunt. We've made these a few too many times!

Bake 375º/8-10 minutes	Makes 3 Dozen (Use medium size scoop)

Ingredients:

2-1/2 cups flour
1 tsp baking soda
1 tsp baking powder
1 tsp salt

1 cup softened butter
¾ cup white sugar
¾ cup brown sugar
2 eggs
1 tsp vanilla

1-1/2 cups mini chocolate chips

Preferably vanilla ice cream

1. Whisk together dry ingredients. Set aside.
2. Beat butter, sugars, eggs, and vanilla for 1 minute.
3. Add dry ingredients.
4. Mix until combined.
5. Add chocolate chips.
6. Mix.
7. Cover a baking sheet with parchment paper.
8. Scoop 1" balls (12 per baking sheet).
9. Bake for 8-10 minutes. Remove from the oven. Let rest on the pan for 5-10 minutes.
10. Fill with 1/3 cup vanilla ice cream.
11. Optional: roll edges in chocolate jimmies.
12. Serve as you make them.

Notes:

- If you are making these ahead of time, do not fill with ice cream until the cookies are completely chilled. Wrap in wax paper and place in an airtight container. Freeze. Yum!!

"Don't let your ice cream melt while you're counting somebody else's sprinkles." _Unknown

"These bars are a velvety lemon dream... perfect addition to a summer party!"
Alaya and Andraya Rumble – Ellensburg, WA

Creamy Lemon Bars

I think of lemon as a summer dessert. It is bright and tangy and makes you feel alive. These bars travel well and are also great for BBQs or parties. Remember, gracious hospitality is good food, but it's also about making your guests feel comfortable and welcome. This doesn't mean everything has to be perfect, just greet them at the door and make them feel at home. This recipe was created in honor of my mother-in-law, Sue, who leads with strength, excitement, and wisdom, and loves lemon!!!!!! Love Heidi!

Bake 325º for 10 Min. + 15 Min.	Makes 9x13

Crust:
2 cups graham cracker crumbs
2 TBSP brown sugar
½ cup melted butter
1/8 tsp salt

1 egg white & 1 TBSP water

Filling:
1 (14oz.) can sweetened-condensed milk
2 whole eggs + 4 egg yolks
1 tsp vanilla

1/3 cup fresh lemon juice
1/3 cup sour cream
1/3 cup whole milk Greek yogurt
1/3 cup sugar

Topping:
2 cups heavy cream
¼ cup powdered sugar

1.) Use blender to crush graham crackers really fine. Mix with brown sugar, melted butter, and salt. Press in bottom of 9x13 pan.
2.) Beat egg white and water and brush over crust. (keeps from getting soggy). Bake 10 minutes.
3.) Beat: sweetened condensed milk, whole eggs, egg yolks, and vanilla.
4.) Add: lemon, sour cream, yogurt, and sugar. Mix till combined. Pour over crust and bake an additional 15 minutes. Will be jiggly in the middle when done.
5.) Let cool 3-4 hours.
6.) Whip cream and spread for the top layer.
7.) Best served very cold.

NOTES:
- With the "egg-white-brush" over the crust, you can make this one day ahead.
- I like to serve in small squares. It is light but rich.

"Rest is not idleness, and to lie sometimes on the grass on a summer day, listening to the murmur of water, or watching the clouds float across the sky, is hardly a waste of time." —John Lubbock

Lemon Meringue Bliss

This dessert is light, airy, and refreshing. The textures are amazing. The meringue gives it a little crunch. The filling is smooth and sweet, and the topping is smooth and tangy. Definitely one of my most favorite desserts I have ever made. You make the crust the night before and leave it in the oven overnight. Make the filling and topping the next day.

Bake 275⁰ 1 hour – leave in oven overnight!	Makes 9x13

Crust:
6 egg whites (save four yolks- for the topping)
1-1/2 cups sugar
½ tsp cream of tartar

Filling:
1 PKG (8 oz.) cream cheese
1/2 cup powdered sugar
1-1/2 cups whipping cream
2 cups mini marshmallows

Topping:
1-1/2 cups of sugar
½ cup cornstarch
2 cups cold water
4 egg yolks

4 TBSP butter
1/3 cup lemon juice

Additional whipping cream for garnish

1.) In mixer beat egg-whites and cream of tartar till foamy. While mixing, slowly add in sugar. Beat till white and glossy. Spread in 9x13 pan lined with parchment.
2.) Bake crust on 275⁰ for 1 hour. When hour is up, shut off oven and leave in the oven 4 hours, or overnight.
3.) FILLING: Soften cream cheese 30 seconds in microwave. Beat cream cheese and powdered sugar. Pour in cream. Beat till fluffy and smooth. Fold in marshmallows. Spread over crust.
4.) TOPPING: In medium bowl whisk egg yolks and set aside.
5.) In saucepan, whisk sugar, cornstarch, and cold water. Bring to a boil, when thick, slowly pour about half the mixture into egg yolks, **Stirring all the while.** *(This keeps eggs from scrambling).*
6.) Stir yolk mixture back into saucepan and boil altogether 1 minute. Remove from heat and add butter and lemon juice. Stir till smooth. Cool 1 hour and spread over filling layer. Refrigerate 4 hours.

NOTES: Lining your pan with parchment is optional but sure saves on the cleanup.

Chocolate Picnic Cookies

If you have ever had the privilege of driving on the Blue Ridge Parkway, then you know the definition of 'picnic' does not include a meal at a picnic table in a designated area. It is pulling your car into the rolling meadows along the road, spreading a big blanket, and pulling out a basket of fried chicken, coleslaw, sweet tea, and chocolate cake. Chocolate cake is a disaster with children, so we whipped up these amazing chocolate cookies.

Bake 375°/8-9 minutes	Makes 3 Dozen (Appx. 1" balls)

Ingredients:

- 2-1/4 cups flour
- 3 TBSP baking cocoa
- 1 (3.4 oz. pkg.) instant chocolate pudding
- ½ tsp salt
- 1 tsp baking soda
- 2 tsp baking powder

- 1 cup softened butter
- ¾ cup brown sugar
- ¼ cup white sugar
- 2 eggs
- 1 tsp vanilla

- 1 cup white chocolate chips
- 1 cup peanut butter chips
- ½ cup white chocolate chips
- Sprinkle of salt

1. Whisk together dry ingredients. Set aside.
2. Beat butter and sugars on high for 1 minute. Time it!
3. Beat in eggs and vanilla, one more minute.
4. Add dry ingredients one cup at a time. Mix.
5. Add chocolate chips. Mix.
6. Cover a baking sheet with parchment paper. Scoop 1" balls.
7. Chop ½ cup white chocolate chips and press into top of cookies. Give a tiny sprinkle of salt.
8. Bake for 8 minutes. Remove from the oven. Let rest on the pan for 5-10 minutes.

Notes:
- Freeze dough balls. Bake as needed.
- If you use this recipe for ice-cream sandwiches, flatten dough balls before baking. Fill with Tillamook® chocolate peanut butter ice cream.

"Pack up the basket, with nice things to eat,
A red and white blanket, to act as our seat.
Cool drinks for drinking, if we get too hot,
It's time for a picnic, let's find the right spot." _AAT

COVER DESSERT
Banana Crème Torte

For some people it's chocolate, for me it's whipped cream. I love whipped cream. The only way whipped cream is better is if it has pudding and something salty with it. This is the kind of dessert you have to throw away if there's leftovers. I could eat a spoonful before lunch, after lunch, and twice before supper. LOL just invite some friends to come share it and whip it up.

Bake crust 425° 12 minutes	Makes 9" Pie or Torte dish

CRUST:
1 cup flour
¼ tsp salt
1 stick butter (refrigerator temp)
3 TBSP ice water

PASTRY CREAM:
4 cups whole milk
2/3 cup sugar
½ tsp salt
1 TBSP vanilla
1/3 cup cornstarch
2 TBSP flour
6 egg yolks
6 TBSP butter

2 Bananas

WHIP CREAM:
2 cups heavy cream
½ cup powdered sugar
½ tsp gelatin (optional)

1-1/2 more bananas for garnish

1.) CRUST: Mix flour and salt. Grate butter into flour on cheese grater. Toss with your hand into a crumble. Add ice water and work with your fingers about 1 minute to form a ball. Let ball rest about 5 minutes and then press into your pan. Poke every ½" with fork holes to reduce shrinkage. Bake till lightly golden brown.

2.) Place milk, sugar, salt, vanilla, cornstarch, and flour in medium saucepan. Whisk.

3.) In separate bowl separate eggs (saves egg whites for something else). Whisk egg yolks.

4.) Bring saucepan with milk and sugar to a boil. When thick, slowly pour about half into egg yolks, whisking all the while. Pour all of it back in saucepan and boil one minute. Take off heat and add butter. Stir till melted. Cool one hour. Spread over crust. Refrigerate 6 hours or overnight.

5.) Garnish with whip cream and bananas.

NOTES:
- You can make this one day ahead if you use the gelatin in whip cream and do not garnish with bananas until you serve. Does not freeze.
- Crust may seem dry when you start forming the ball, but as the butter softens it will be enough moisture. There is enough butter you don't have to roll it out.

"The older you get, the better you are. Unless you are a banana." _Betty White

"Cappuccino Fluff was definitely a hit for my sister's birthday. It was easy to put together the night before, and the espresso gave the fluff the depth of flavor that brought you back for more,"
Carmela Lopez – Fargo, ND

Cappuccino Fluff

This is always a potluck pleaser. If I bring this somewhere, I always bring my bowl back home empty. Bring little cups or bowls to serve it in. You can use Cool Whip instead of whipped cream, but, if you get in the habit of buying cream it is much better for you. Whipped cream is not hard to make. You don't need to chill your bowl………. Just follow this recipe and mix it up.

No cooking required.	Makes 2 quarts.

Ingredients:

- 1/3 cup hot water
- 3 TBSP instant coffee

- 3-1/2 cups milk
- 1 large box instant chocolate pudding

- 1 (8oz.) pkg. cream cheese
- ½ cup powdered sugar
- 2 cups whipping cream

- 1 pkg regular Oreos

1.) In large bowl, whisk together water and coffee, until dissolved. Add in milk and pudding and stir till smooth. Set aside.
2.) Crush Oreos. Reserve ½ cup crumbs for garnish.
3.) Soften cream cheese for 30 seconds in microware. Place in mixing bowl with powdered sugar and whipping cream. Whip until mixture forms a nice stiff cream (yes, you can whip the cream and cream cheese at the same time).
4.) Fold cream mixture and Oreos into coffee pudding. Stir just enough to combine but still leave streaks of white and brown. Sprinkle the rest of the cookies on top. Refrigerate.

NOTES:

- Can be made one day in advance.
- For extra goodness! Use 6 shots of expresso (instead of instant). 😊 (Do not add 1/3 cup hot water)
- Make a double batch and reserve two little jars for you and daddy to eat in bed after prayers.

"Behind every successful person, is a substantial amount of coffee." _Unknown

Raspberry Crumble Bars

Mark this as QUICK, you can make this in 15 minutes or less. Absolutely delicious and a favorite. I remember being a new bride in New Ipswich and my late Mother-in-law would make something like this. I wish I would have gotten her recipe. FYI, be the best mother-in-law you can. Mine treated me like her own daughter, even her memory warms my heart.

| Bake 350° 28 Minutes | Makes 9x13 – Serve Cold |

Crumble (Reserve 1/3 for topping):
- 1-1/2 cups butter
- 1-1/2 cups brown sugar
- 3 cups flour
- 3 cups oatmeal
- 1 tsp baking powder
- 1-1/4 tsp salt

Cream Cheese Layer:
- 2 (8oz.) packages cream cheese
- 1 cup sugar
- 2 eggs
- 2 tsp vanilla

Filling:
- ¾ cup cold water
- 3 TBSP cornstarch
- 3 TBSP sugar
- 1-1/2 cup raspberries

1.) CRUMBLE: Soften butter. Add all other ingredients and with a fork stir into a crumble.
2.) Spread two-thirds of the crumble into a greased 9x13 and press down.
3.) CREAM CHEESE LAYER: Soften cream cheese. Mix to smooth out lumps. Add sugar, eggs, and vanilla. Whip 2 minutes and spread over crust.
4.) FILLING: In small saucepan, put water, sugar, and cornstarch. Whisk out any lumps. Add raspberries. Bring to a boil. Pour hot berries over cream cheese. It's ok if it's a little clumpy.
5.) Sprinkle remaining crumble. Press down slightly.
6.) Bake till slightly golden.

NOTES:
- Bars freeze well. Thaw at room temperature.
- I recommend making these bars the day before. They are better after sitting and they are best served very cold.
- For the berry filling, you can also use 4 TBSP raspberry jam and 1-1/3 cup fresh raspberries. No need to heat.

"The sweet doesn't end up in the stomach, the sweet goes straight to the heart." _Unknown

Birthday Cake Squares

This recipe happened without trying and stuck. My Father-In-Law was visiting, it was his birthday, I needed something I could put a candle in, and he doesn't eat much sugar. It was also strawberry season and he loves strawberries. Bingo, these were the ingredients on hand. A year later when our granddaughter turned one, Linn asked me, "What was that dessert you made for grandpa's birthday? It was the best thing ever, I want to make it for Kalli."

No baking	9x13 12-20 servings

Crust:
1 package white Oreos
(no substituting)
½ cup butter

Ice Cream:
½ gallon vanilla ice cream
½ gallon strawberry ice cream
Recommend Tillamook

Garnish:
Fresh berries
Spray whip cream

1.) Line pan with parchment. This will allow you to lift dessert out and cut before serving.
2.) Crush Oreos.
3.) Melt butter and combine with Oreo's. Press in bottom of 9x13.
4.) Layer vanilla ice cream.
5.) Layer strawberry ice cream.
6.) Cut dessert.
7.) Poke in popsicle sticks.
8.) Cover and freeze.
9.) Recut before serving.

NOTES:
- Can be made as far in advance as you need.
- Can also be made in a round 10" cake pan. Using the parchment paper, lift it out of the pan and place on a cake stand. Cut in pie shaped pieces.
- Optional: Garnish with berries of your choice.
- Tillamook Ice cream is readily available and is our favorite. If you can't find it in your area, only replace with good quality ice cream. Not all strawberry ice cream is good.
- FYI a half gallon of ice-cream is the WHOLE carton!

"Age is an issue of mind over matter. If you don't mind, it doesn't matter." _Mark Twain

Hot Fudge Topping

This recipe is not original to me. It is here as a place of honor to my grandmother. The first pages of this book were written on the airplane, as I made my last trip to visit her. She now is where we all hope to be, Praise the Lord!! And I have memories to sustain me for a lifetime. This recipe is one of those memories. It goes like this: Sunday afternoon, everyone at Gran and Pa's because they always loved company, sitting on the back porch, eating dessert, and the airplanes to PDX droning overhead. I can't resist adding that Pa always had to try all the ice cream flavors in the same bowl and then cover it in fudge sauce.

Stovetop	Makes about 2 cups

Ingredients:

- ½ cup butter
- 1 cup chocolate chips
- 1 tsp vanilla
- 2 cups powdered sugar
- 1 can evaporated milk

1. In saucepan, melt butter and chocolate chips.
2. Add vanilla, powdered sugar, and evaporated milk.
3. Bring to a boil. Boil about 8 minutes.
4. Cool before serving.
5. Store in tightly covered jar in refrigerator.
6. Microwave whenever you want to reuse.

NOTES:

- When reheating in microwave, stir every 30 seconds.
- Store up to 3 months in fridge.

"A grandmother is warm hugs and sweet memories. She remembers all your accomplishments and forgets all your mistakes." _Barbara Cage

"A grandmother is a little bit parent, a little bit teacher, a little bit best friend." _Southern Living

Old-Fashioned Shortcake

I come from a family that thinks of "shortcake" as a modern version of sponge-cake, ice cream, and mashed berries; that's good too, but I love the original version. In England, in the 1500's "Short" meant "Crumbly" and shortcake was served as a crumbly biscuit similar to a scone; this was achieved by adding fat to the flour to break up the gluten strands. The simplicity and beauty of this old-fashioned dessert appeals to me for its delicate textures, colors, and assembly of wholeness. It shines best with the freshest fruit of the season.

Bake 400° for 14 minutes	Makes 8

Ingredients:

- 2 cups flour
- 3 TBSP cornstarch
- 1 TBSP baking powder
- ¼ tsp soda
- 4 TBSP sugar
- 1 tsp salt

- ½ cup butter (1 stick)

- ¾ cup milk
- 2 tsp vinegar

- 3 TBSP Sugar in the Raw

- Fruit
- 2 cups whipping cream
- ½ cup powdered sugar
- 1 tsp vanilla

1.) Line baking sheet with parchment paper.
2.) Pour vinegar into milk and set aside.
3.) Combine flour, cornstarch, baking powder, soda, sugar, and salt. Whisk together.
4.) Use a cheese grater to grate butter into flour mixture. Toss the grated butter evenly into flour using your fingers or a fork.
5.) Pour milk mixture into flour and combine with a large spoon. Dump out dough onto countertop and press into a 9" circle. Cut into 8 pieces.
6.) Sprinkle 1 TBSP of sugar onto parchment and place biscuits on sheet. Sprinkle with remaining sugar. Bake. Check at 12 minutes.
7.) Whip cream with powdered sugar and vanilla.
8.) May serve warm.

NOTES:

- You can make these one day ahead.
- Bake just until edges are lightly browned.
- Serve with whipped cream and fruit of your choice.

"Let your energy be used to build, not destroy" _Unknown

Chocolate Cheesecake Bars

These are the "Hubby" bars. Brandon loves chocolate, like how "chocolate-lovers" love chocolate. He also loves cheesecake. With these bars we were trying for a blend of both. Our husbands would tell you to pair them with black coffee. At the last family gathering my dad asked what we were doing with the leftovers, he said, "I could take them home." We put them on a plate, then he said, "I think I will eat them right now!"

Bake 325° 10 minutes + 25-27 Minutes	Makes 9x13

Crust:
2-1/2 cups regular Oreos (this is 24 cookies, crush in blender)
1/3 cup melted butter
1/8 tsp salt

Cheesecake Filling:
8 oz. cream cheese
1 can (14oz.) sweetened condensed milk
6 eggs
½ cup whole milk Greek yogurt
1 tsp vanilla
½ cup sugar
1/3 cup cocoa powder

Chocolate Ganache:
½ cup heavy cream
½ cup semi-sweet chips
½ cup milk chocolate chips

Whipped Cream:
2 cups heavy cream
1/3 cup powdered sugar

1.) Crush Oreos and mix with melted butter and salt. Press in bottom of 9x13 pan. Bake 10 minutes.
2.) Soften cream cheese 30 seconds in micro. Beat with sweetened condensed milk until smooth.
3.) While mixing, add eggs one at a time. Add yogurt, vanilla, sugar, and baking cocoa.
4.) Spread filling over crust and bake for 25-30 minutes. Let cool 1 hour before adding ganache.
5.) GANACHE: melt cream and chocolate chips in microwave stirring every 30 seconds. When smooth, pour over baked cheesecake. Refrigerate 5 hours or overnight.
6.) Prepare and spread whipped cream over chilled bars.

NOTES:
- Do not use "double stuff" Oreos. It is overpowering.
- I usually make this dessert the day before and just add the whipped cream right before I serve it.
- Must serve chilled.

Grilled Blueberry Crisp

This dessert has New England roots 25 years deep. When my best friend Lisa worked as editor for Yankee Magazine, she would often test recipes on the weekends. I had a great kitchen and she had great recipes and together we made the best memories! This was the beginning of a whole new chapter in cooking for me. We made everything from raspberry tarts to scallops and mussels. I remember when she showed up with a jar of capers, I thought things were going too far.

Medium Heat/Bake 375° 35 minutes	Makes 10" iron skillet

Ingredients:
- 6 cups blueberries
- ¼ cups flour
- ½ cups sugar

Topping:
- 1 cup flour
- ½ cup oats
- ¾ cup brown sugar
- 1 stick butter, softened
- ½ tsp salt
- ½ tsp cinnamon
- ¼ tsp ginger

1.) Spray cast iron skillet with non-stick cooking spray.
2.) Mix berries, flour, and sugar. Toss to coat and spread in skillet.
3.) TOPPING: Combine flour, oats, sugar, butter, salt, cinnamon, and ginger. Stir with hand mixer or pastry blender until crumbly.
4.) Spread over berries and bake.
5.) I put all the burners on the gas grill on medium; that's about 350-375. Cook until bubbling and topping is lightly browned.
6.) You may cook in the oven. I just love the smoky smell from the grill.

NOTES:
- You may use a 9x13 disposable aluminum pan. This grills just fine.
- Don't use glass pans on the grill.
- Best eaten the same day as made.
- Best eaten when still warm and served with vanilla ice cream.
- Frozen berries work great too; add 10 minutes to cook time.

"The blueberries in Sal's pail went kerplink, kerplank, kerplunk" _Robert McCloskey
Taken from the children's book *Blue Berries for Sal*. Possibly the sweetest children's book ever written.

Chocolate Chip Cookie Bars

Sometimes "Less is more" or "Simple is best". You really can't beat a good chocolate chip cookie. These are my go-to church bars. I can whip them up Sunday morning and let them bake while I'm making breakfast. I do like to be more organized than that, but life happens. This is a great way to still be able to bring something homemade in a short amount of time.

Bake 350º 24 minutes	Makes 9x13

Ingredients:

- ¾ cup butter
- 1 cup white sugar
- ¼ cup brown sugar
- 1 tsp vanilla
- 3 eggs

- 1 tsp salt
- 1-1/2 tsp baking powder
- ½ tsp soda
- 3-1/2 cups flour

- 1 cup mini chocolate chips
- 1 cup chocolate chips

1.) Mix butter, sugar, and vanilla. Whip one minute. Beat in eggs one at a time (turns cream color when whipped enough).
2.) Add dry ingredients. Mix.
3.) Add chocolate chips. Mix.
4.) Line 9x13 with parchment.
5.) Spread dough in pan. I press it in with my hands. Bake until center puffs up and slightly brown around the edges. They are best if the center is just chewy.
6.) Cool. Cut. Store.

NOTES:

- They freeze well.
- Mix and match chocolate chips with: Toffee bits, caramel bits, nuts, marshmallows, M&M's, coconut….. You get the idea.
- Go all out with a scoop of vanilla ice cream and some hot fudge sauce from this chapter. Gourmet! Simple amazing goodness!

"Raisin Cookies that look like Chocolate Chip are the main reason I have trust issues." _Woody Paige

Chocolate Skillet Cake

Our life is a collection of memories, and a lot of those memories are a combination of nuances around us. You might have fond memories of "Game Night" at home, but what you are really remembering is: Loving family, friendships, candles burning, rain dripping, piano playing, and maybe pop-corn, (Diet Coke if at dad and mom's). Here is a new one to add to that list. Chocolate Skillet cake cooking in the oven, waiting to be eaten before it's cool enough to frost.

Bake 350º - Bake 27 minutes	Makes 10" skillet

Ingredients:
1-1/2 cups flour
1-1/2 cups sugar
½ cup baking cocoa
1-1/2 tsp soda
½ tsp baking powder
½ tsp salt

2/3 cup buttermilk
1/3 cup oil
2 eggs
1-1/2 tsp vanilla
2/3 cup warm water

Ganache:
1/3 cup cream
2/3 cups chocolate chips

Chocolate Whip Cream:
2 cups heavy cream
¼ cup baking cocoa
½ cup powdered sugar
1 tsp vanilla

1.) Spray 10" cast iron skillet with cooking spray.
2.) Mix dry ingredients in a bowl and set aside.
3.) Place all wet ingredients in a bowl and whisk together. Add to dry ingredients. Stir to combine. Pour in skillet. Bake 27 minutes or until toothpick comes out mostly clean.
4.) Cool 1 hour.
5.) GANACHE: melt cream and chocolate chips in a microwave proof bowl, stirring every 30 seconds. Pour over cake.
6.) WHIPPED CREAM: Place cream cocoa, sugar, and vanilla in blender or mixer. Whip till soft peaks form. Spread or pipe over ganache layer.

NOTES:
- If you want to make ahead of time, add 1 tsp plain gelatin to whip cream to stabilize.
- For a simple edition, serve warm cake with ice cream.

"Chocolate cake – the backbone of desserts" _AAT

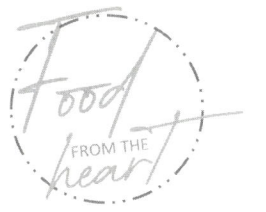

Carrot Cake
CREAM CHEESE & BROWNED BUTTER ICING

Carrot cake is just like a glue for friendship!! Everyone should make a good carrot cake, and every cake should be shared with friends. When we started talking about a carrot cake recipe for this book, I couldn't believe all the great places I've shared carrot cake with friends: The Table in Asheboro, Open Road in Tryon, Maxie "B's" in Greensboro(NC), DB Dessert Company in Portland(OR), to Gibbit Hill Grill in Groton(MA)………

Bake 350° - 28 minutes	Makes 9x13 glass pan

Cake Layer:
2-1/4 cup flour
1-1/2 tsp baking powder
1 tsp soda
1 tsp salt
1-1/2 tsp cinnamon
½ tsp nutmeg

1-1/4 cups oil
1 cup brown sugar
1 cup white sugar
4 large eggs
1 TBSP vanilla

3 cups carrots
1 cup chopped pecans (optional)

Frosting:
½ cup butter (browned)
1 pkg (8oz.) cream cheese
¼ cup heavy cream
1/8 tsp salt
6 cups powdered sugar

1.) Spray pan.
2.) Mix all dry ingredients. Set aside.
3.) Beat oil, sugars, eggs, and vanilla, two minutes.
4.) Add dry ingredients. Mix to combine.
5.) CARROTS: I use 3 cups baby carrots. Blend/food processor till finely shredded but still small pieces. Fold carrots into cake batter.
6.) If adding nuts, chop finely and fold into batter.
7.) Pour batter into greased pan.
8.) Bake till toothpick comes out clean. Do not overbake. Cool cake in pan, on rack.
9.) FROSTING: in small frying pan melt butter. Melt till butter is light brown. Place butter and all frosting ingredients in mixer. Beat three minutes. Set aside till cake and frosting are cool.

NOTES:
- For a layer cake: Bake in 3 (8" rounds). Bake appx. 22 minutes. This recipe makes enough frosting to frost the cake and a thin filling between layers (1/3 cup). Use parchment circles in the bottom of pans, for easy release. The parchment is a miracle when frosting, as there are no crumbs.

KNOW YOUR CAKE

Cake is done when it slightly pulls away from the side of the pan.

Cake is done when a toothpick comes out with no batter on it.

Cake is done when you press down lightly, and it springs back.

Cake is done when the internal temperature is between 205° -210°.

Index

A
Apple Pie Scones 49
Asian Crunch Salad 65

B
Baked Haddock with Crab Stuffing 165
Banana Crème Torte (Cover) 182
Basil Aioli 158
Best Oven Fries 91
Birthday Cake Squares 189
Blueberry Strata 46
Breakfast Fusions 56
Beef:
    Beef Enchiladas 123
    Cheeseburger Soup 138
    French Dip with Au Jus 137
    Homemade Stroganoff 141
    Korean Beef 130
    Salisbury Steaks 133
    Sloppy Joe Bowls 134
    Slow Cooked Short Ribs 129
    Steak Tacos 108

C
Cappuccino Fluff 185
Carnitas 112
Carrot Cake 202
Celebrate Everything Cupcakes 173
Cheeseburger Soup 138
Cheese Dunkers 83
Chicken Citrus Soak 101
Chicken:
    Chicken BLT Wedge Salad 62
    Chicken Enchiladas 124
    Chicken Gyro 157
    Chicken Parmesan 161
    Chicken Pie 154
    Chicken Taquitos 119
    Chicken Scampi 153
    Chicken Tacos 107
    Friday Night Chicken Sandwich 163
    Garlic Chicken Caesar Wraps 142
    Sticky Chicken 150

Chocolate:
    Cappuccino Fluff 185
    Chocolate Cheesecake Bars 195
    Chocolate Chip Cookie Bars 198
    Chocolate Picnic Cookies 181
    Chocolate Skillet Cake 201
    Creamy Lemon Bars 17
Crescent Rolls 87
Crockpot Ham 145
Croutons 70

D
Darling Dutch Babies 26

E
Egg Bites 50

F
French Dip with Au Jus 137
Fish/Seafood:
    Baked Haddock with Crab Stuffing ... 165
    Honey Sriracha Shrimp 166
    Shrimp Tacos 111
Fluffy Fruit Dip 45

G
Garlic Chicken Caesar Wraps 142
Grilled Blueberry Crisp 197

H
Heidi's Bread 84
Homemade Caesar Salad 70
Homemade Guacamole 116
Homemade Queso 115
Homemade Stroganoff 141
Honey Balsamic w/ Parmesan Crisps 69
Honey Sriracha Shrimp 166
Hot Honey BBQ 101
Hot Fudge Topping 191

I
Ice Cream Sandwiches 174

J
Japanese Steakhouse White Sauce 96

K
Korean BBQ Sauce 97
Korean Beef 130

Index

L

Lasagna Soup 149
Lemon Meringue Bliss 178

M

Megas Supreme 29
Mom's Jello Salad 81
Mo's Salad 75

N

No-Bake Granola 33
North Carolina BBQ Sauce 97

O

Old Fashioned Shortcake 192
Old Saylor's Veggie Dip 77
Olive Garden from Scratch 72
Overnight French Toast 30

P

Pasta:
    Chicken Parmesan 161
    Chicken Scampi 153
    Sausage Tortellini Bake 146
Pecan Rolls 37
Perfect Mashed Potatoes 88
Pop Tarts 54
Pork/Sausage:
    Carnitas 112
    Crockpot Ham 145
    Sausage Tortellini Bake 146
Potatoes:
    Perfect Mashed Potatoes 88
    Best Oven Fries 91

Q

R

Raspberry Crumble Bars 186
Roasted Carrots 78
Rub 101 98
Rub for the Beef 99
Rub for the Birds 98
Rub for the Pig 99
Running Balls 38

S

Salisbury Steaks 133
Sausage Tortellini Bake 146
School Pancakes 41
Shrimp Tacos 111
Sloppy Joe Bowls 134
Slow Cooked Short Ribs 129
Smoothie Bowls 34
Special Kale Salad 66
Steak Tacos 108
Sticky Chicken 150
Sweet Potato Feta Bowls 42
Salad:
    Asian Crunch Salad 65
    BLT Wedge Salad 62
    Friday Night Chicken Sandwich 163
    Homemade Caesar 70
    Honey Balsamic w/ Parmesan Crisps 69
    Mo's Salad 75
    Olive Garden From Scratch 72
    Special Kale Salad 66
Salad Dressing ....
Sandwiches:
    Blue Ridge Club 158
    Chicken Gyro 157
    Garlic Chicken Caesar Wraps 142
    The Brunch Sandwich 25
Smoothies 34
Soup:
    Cheeseburger Soup 138
    Lasagna Soup 149
Sticky Chicken w Pineapple Rice 150

T

Taco Bowls 120
Tartar Sauce 96
The Brunch Sandwich 25
Tomato Basil Quiche 53
Topping Off Marinade 100

U

V

Author's Notes

1.) Baking/ cooking times are for an electric stove. Gas can really vary.
2.) Recipes are tested with olive oil, avocado oil, and vegetable oil.
3.) We only use pink Himalayan salt.
4.) We only use quality flour such as: "King Arthur", "Bread Flour", or "Restaurant" flour.
5.) Store flour in an airtight container.
6.) Always shake once before use.
7.) Always measure with a cup and level with a knife.
8.) We only use Fleischmann's® instant dry yeast.
9.) Replace your baking soda, baking powder and yeast every two months.
10.) Test your oven temperature – Walmart sells an oven thermometer for under $5.00.
11.) For simple pleasures that don't really cost extra, buy: "Coarse ground black pepper"! This allows you to add pepper flavor without turning your food gray. Also, buy "Coarse" salt. This pleases your tastebuds without over-salting your food.
12.) A few recipes call for jalapeño juice. This is just the juice found in minced or sliced jalapeños, found with the pickles at your grocery store.
13.) Always keep a sink of hot soapy water and clean up as you cook.

Food From the Heart was founded in 2018, by two sisters who share a passion for: God and country, marriage, homemaking, hospitality, family-life, cooking, children, and beautiful things.

Ann Traffie (Left) Stay at home mom of 13, wife to Dave, Grandma to 3, how FUN!!! Her days are filled with multiplication and division, kissing boo-boos, and crunching numbers for their family home-building business. The best days are normal ones, that end with a date night, think: Hubby, iced coffee, good conversations, and possibly a new book. Although ambitious, she doesn't forget to slow down, light a candle in the kitchen, and dream up scrumptious food to keep those little bottomless tummies full.

Heidi Matson (Right) Stay at home mom of three, now a GIRL mom too!!! Wife to Brandon, saved by grace, recovering professional procrastinator, and wanna-be cool homeschool mom. Heidi loves festive holidays and finds the magic moments in everyday life, inspiring. She chooses to have lots of white walls to scrub and smiles at the thought of the little hands that left the prints. Although date nights and family-adventurers give her much delight, being at home, preferably windows open, children playing, and coffee in hand, her kitchen is her favorite spot.

We so enjoyed our readers feedback from Book One, we hope to hear from you again. Please feel free to email us at the following. foodfromtheheartcookbook@gmail.com